Stradey Stories

Alun Wyn Bevan

Gomer

Sincere thanks to:
- Jill, my long suffering wife, for her help and support.
- to Gomer Press for the invitation to compile this volume.
- to Huw Evans, Les Williams, David Jones, Clifford Bowen Samuel, Rob Lewis, Ray Williams, Lisa Alvarez Kairelis, John Harris, Janet Evans, Ray Gravell, Gareth Charles, Harry Howells, Wenna Davies, Clive John, Neil McIlroy, Bethan Clement, Jacqui Price, Claire Price, Alan T. Richards and Adrian Howells for their willingness to help.

Picture Acknowledgements

Huw Evans Picture Agency: 87, 89, 116, 121, 123, 128, 132, 137, 148, 150, 151, 153, 154, 156, 161, 167, 170, 175, 182, 183, 184, 185, 188, 198. Les Williams: 31, 61, 79, 102, 106, 126, 129, 139, 141, 147, 149, 152, 167, 185, 196. John Harris: 93, 94, 114. Robert Evans: 35, 37. Inpho Photography (Dublin): 162. David Jones: 143. Clifford Bowen Samuel:135. Alan T. Richards: 131. Illustrated London News Picture Library: 108. Jim Gittings: 158.

Every effort has been made to contact the copyright holders of all the pictures in this book. Gomer Press would be only too glad to receive any information about pictures whose sources we have been unable to credit.

In memory of
William Aldwyn and Rachel Anne Williams, two enthusiastic followers.

First Impression – 2005
Second Impression – 2005

ISBN 1 84323 570 6 (softback)
ISBN 1 84323 647 8 (hardback)

Printed in Wales by
Gomer Press, Llandysul, Ceredigion

Contents

Foreword

'Beware your dreams: they might come true!'

Little did I think, as a timid and skinny five-year-old boy perched on my father's sturdy shoulders, that I too would play for the Scarlets at Stradey Park. Stradey Park! Now, that's where my imagination was fuelled and fired to the brink of obsession. That's where a dream was born that I never truly thought would be realised.

It all began way back in the Fifties when my father, Jack Gravell, a collier at Pentremawr Colliery in the Gwendraeth Valley, took me to Stradey to watch Llanelli play. A former wing forward himself who had played for the top West Wales clubs, Cydweli and Pontyberem, my father was a tough man who enjoyed his rugby immensely. His dream was that his son Raymond (that's me) would one day play for Wales as he had once dreamed of doing.

His words will stay with me forever: '*Dere mlân, ni'n mynd lan i Strade!*' And off we went: me with my hero; he and his friends supporting their heroes, who eventually became my heroes. Now I can't recall who won the game, I can't even remember the name of the other team, but I can remember vividly the field, the wooden stand, the crowd, the noise, the excitement and, of course, the players, who seemed so far away to the inquisitive eyes of a tiny boy.

We eventually got home to the village of Mynydd y Garreg, some nine miles from Llanelli, via a bus journey to the nearby town of Cydweli before tramping the last mile on foot to home and happiness.

All these memories came flooding back to me (as did the tears!) as I read the 'Stradey Stories', beautifully penned with passion and purpose by the author Alun Wyn Bevan.

My father introduced me to Stradey and Llanelli RFC and I can proudly say that I did realise my dream: I played for Llanelli, I played at Stradey. I actually captained the club and was the youngest member of the team that beat the mighty All Blacks of New Zealand by nine points to three on the Tuesday afternoon of October 31, 1972.

To play for Wales was one step beyond my wildest dream. But on January 18, 1975 at Parc des Princes, Paris, I realised my father's dream: I played for Wales!

My father died when I was fourteen years of age, but on the afternoon of my first cap, he was there; he carried me through that game shoulder high as he had done when I was a little boy with my hero at Stradey Park. *Diolch* Dad and *diolch* Alun, for making our dreams once again come true.

Ray Gravell   President, Llanelli Scarlets

Introduction

The Llanelli Scarlets have been called the Manchester United of the rugby world. But even though it's the home of football's Red Devils, Old Trafford, that's known as 'The Theatre of Dreams', for me and countless youngsters from the Gwendraeth Valley back in the 1970s (and I dare say for generations before and since), there was only one theatre of dreams – Stradey Park.

One of my earliest memories of the ground is being smuggled in under the coat of a season-ticket holder to see the old Floodlit Alliance games or to witness the visit of 'foreigners' such as the Harlequins, Coventry and Bath in their battle for the old rag doll swinging from one of the Stradey crossbars. So you can imagine the sheer delight and excitement of playing at Stradey Park for Mynydd Mawr under-11s against Llanelli under-11s and actually using the same changing room and running down the same tunnel as some of my heroes. Now that really was living the dream. For that instant I WAS Delme Thomas, Derek Quinnell or Phil Bennett, and nobody and nothing can ever take that magic moment away from me.

Visits by international touring teams to Stradey Park were such auspicious occasions that we were given a half-day holiday in Gwendraeth Grammar School and given official permission therefore to be part of such legendary events as the conquering of the mighty All Blacks in 1972 or the unforgettable 28-all draw against Australia in 1978. When the Scarlets were in their heyday, Max Boyce's words certainly rang true – 'All roads led to Stradey Park' – and I can proudly echo Max's sentiment that indeed 'I was there.'

The seven-mile bus trip from my home in Ponthenri to Llanelli became a weekly pilgrimage to be amongst the vociferous mob on the Tanner Bank, where experiencing all the banter from the crowd was almost as important as the rugby itself. Mind you, Llanelli supporters – much like those of Manchester United – aren't always appreciated outside their own region. A question often asked in other rugby grounds across Wales 'What do you call a Llanelli supporter with two eyes?' and the answer of course is 'Twins!' I hope I've spent enough time at Stradey to be forgiven that old chestnut. And, anyway, experience in Wales and throughout the world tells me that it's not just Scarlet supporters that fall into the one-eyed category by a long, long chalk.

But if a youngster managed to live a dream by treading the hallowed turf of Stradey Park, then for a man made worldly-wise and more than a touch cynical by years in the hyped-up world of modern media, having a dream come true was to spend countless hours in the company of players I'd grown up regarding as heroes. In over 20 years working for the BBC on radio and television, it's been nothing short of a pleasure and privilege not just working alongside but being in the company of the likes of Phil Bennett, J.J. Williams, Ray Gravell and more latterly Ieuan Evans, Jonathan Davies and Gwyn Jones, to name just a few. On trips to Europe and beyond, it's a joy to be with these former players as they recount tales of past characters and events, evoking the serious and the sad, the sublime and the ridiculous.

Of all the characters that have graced Stradey Park over the years, few have entered its folklore quite like the incomparable Ray Gravell. A larger-than-life character who readily makes himself the butt of the joke, Ray recalls with fondness incidents like one game at Stradey Park where he was left grimacing in pain having twisted his ankle after a particularly heavy tackle. Onto the field rushed arguably the best known trainer of the time, Bert Peel (grandfather of the current Scarlets and Wales scrum half, Dwayne Peel). While Grav was clutching his injured leg, Bert applied the magic sponge to the bearded wonder's head.

'But Bert,' said Grav in his native Welsh, 'this is where the pain is.'

Calmly, and with his customary smile, Bert answered,

'That's as may be Grav *bach*. But this is where the problem is!"

That's the kind of story, complemented by the usual abundance of facts unearthed by Alun Wyn Bevan, that will live on thanks to this book. The book is published as the Scarlets prepare to move from their spiritual home at Stradey Park to a brand new stadium on the other side of town. It's very apt therefore that the memories and legends collected in over a century are recorded for posterity. The bricks and mortar, the fixtures and fittings may well disappear, but the spirit of Stradey will live on forever. For the next generation of Scarlets, the theatre may be new but the dream will be the same.

Gareth Charles   Rugby Correspondent BBC Wales

The author (left), Jonathan Davies and Gareth Charles in Pretoria, 1998.

1

How the Love Affair Began

Childhood recollections

Call me sentimental – and believe me, my son does – but I can't help thinking that my boyhood days were halcyon ones. After all, to live in Brynaman in the 1950s and 1960s was to be at the centre of the universe. Why, there were 56 shops along Station Road alone, stocking every conceivable item necessary for day-to-day living. In fact, a journey to the nearby towns of Swansea, Neath and Llanelli was only contemplated if a major purchase, such as a new MG Magnette or a Rayburn, was imminent.

Granted, those West Wales bastions of first-class sport, The Vetch, St Helen's and Stradey Park, were only a short drive away. But, our theatre of dreams in those days was the field at the bottom end of Bryn Avenue. Our heroes weren't Don Shepherd, Terry Davies or Ivor Allchurch; we idolised Ossie Evans, Tyssul Thomas and John Brinley Davies! We didn't feel it necessary to abandon these young men and widen our horizons.

Indeed the only time we felt able to tear ourselves away from our very own Wembley was when we embarked on the annual Sunday School Outing to Tenby. Wickets were immediately pitched on the town's South Beach within striking distance of the Atlantic Ocean!

There were exceptions to this self-imposed rule, of course. Now, if one of our local lads happened to be playing on permit for Swansea, Neath or Llanelli, then carloads of supporters would make the journey to support him. The 'permit' arrangement went something like this: if one of the regular first-class players was unavailable due to injury, a promising 'rising star' from a team such as Brynaman would be drafted in to play for the bigger club. This could happen on several occasions during a given season without compromising the individual or the local village team – as long as they didn't play more than five games. This meant that he was still a Brynaman player even if he did wear the scarlet of Llanelli. Thus it was that Huw Harries of Amman United, Raymond Jones of Brynaman or Gordon Reed of Cwmgors would find themselves running out at Stradey on a Saturday afternoon. And we lads would be there to support our local hero and not neccessarily the Llanelli team!

Once the game was over it was a mad dash home to report how well John Elgar Williams had played at fullback or, on one occasion, how Ken Pugh had won the game single-handedly for Swansea in the dying minutes at Stradey with a deft dropped goal from a scrummage in the shadow of the Llanelli posts. News such as this spread around the village like wildfire so that there

Brynaman's John Elgar with his Llanelli team-mates, 1962–63.

Back row (left to right): Brian Davies, Colin Elliott, Marlston Morgan, Delme Thomas, Tony Macdonald, John Warlow, Norman Gale, John Elgar Williams.

Middle row (left to right): Arthur Davies (secretary), Gwyn Robins, Barrie Jackson, Bryan Thomas (captain), Elvet Jones (chairman), Dennis Thomas, Robert Morgan.

Front row (left to right): Stuart Davies, Freddie Bevan.

would be no need to tune into the BBC Welsh Home Service for the sports report just prior to the epilogue.

While there was pride at the prospect of a local boy playing for the senior club, our main priority was still the village team. We were far more interested in the clashes between Brynaman and Amman United, or Cwmllynfell and Cwmgors, than anything that went on at Twickenham or the Arms Park. Yes, it was a black day if Wales lost to Ireland, but it was a disaster of cataclysmic proportions if Brynaman lost at Llandybie.

Over the years the relationship between the village sides and Llanelli Rugby Club has evolved into a very close one. I have fond memories of being taken by my father and grandfather to Stradey. We would have to walk what seemed like miles from a muddy lane in the vicinity to queue at the ticket booth. As we inched anxiously forward, we wondered whether there would be enough tickets left for us to buy. Once inside we would stand patiently on the Tanner Bank waiting for the game to start. And when the half-time whistle had been blown, there was a mad rush to get onto the field to practise some passing or kicking manoeuvres. At the conclusion of play we would sprint on again, this time with autograph books at the ready. Once home, the hallowed match programme was neatly filed away with others on the boxroom shelves, with orders not to touch! When I look back on those times I am amazed at the sheer numbers of people who supported unstintingly. The streets were awash with supporters and every square inch of parking space taken up with cars.

It was a wonderful, thrilling experience being part of the crowd. How much more exhilarating it must have beeen to don the scarlet shirt of Llanelli! Yes, I am a sentimentalist and I know that the young men of my generation from Brynaman and the surrounding area would have given anything to do just that.

2

'We're not playing!'

The first international played at Stradey Park

Stradey Park, St Helen's, The Gnoll, Cardiff Arms Park, Rodney Parade, Eugene Cross Park, Ynysangharad Park – names to conjure with for rugby and cricket followers the length and breadth of Wales; venues that have hosted some of the great sporting confrontations.

During the winter months Cardiff Arms Park would bear witness to Wilfred Wooller's prowess in the red jersey of Wales, or the blue and black of Cardiff. Come April, however, the aforesaid Mr Wooller could be seen striding forth purposefully to the wicket in his pristine white cricket flannels representing Glamorgan County Cricket Club.

At Rodney Parade tales are still told of the John Uzzell drop goal which secured a narrow victory for Newport over Wilson Whineray's All Blacks in 1963. It was also at Rodney Parade that Emrys Davies scored an unbeaten 287 and Walter Hammond a magnificent 309 during the glorious summer of 1939, a week before Hitler declared war in Europe.

The Gnoll at Neath was the spiritual home of the giants of the Neath and Dulais valleys. Roy John, Morlais Williams, Rees Stephens and Brian Thomas were the rugby-playing heroes, while Len Muncer (8-48 against Somerset in 1949) and Steve Barwick (5-63 in a one-day game in 1994) excelled with the hard, red, round ball.

The supporters at Eugene Cross Park at Ebbw Vale were treated to some unforgettable rugby thanks to Wilf Hunt, Glyn Turner and Clive Burgess, whilst Len Pitchford, Wilf Hughes and Jack Cope provided the entertainment on the cricket square (weather permitting!).

Of all the areas which have played host to both sports, surely one of the most aesthetically-pleasing playing fields has to be Ynysangharad Park at Pontypridd. Sadly, the rugby ground has been reduced in size and eventually relocated as a result of the A470 which bypasses the town. But the cricket arena lives on. It is set amongst picturesque parkland and surrounded by the reclaimed greenery of the overlooking mountains, so I am always amazed at the cricketer's ability to concentrate on the job in hand and not stand awhile and admire the view.

But Stradey Park may well have the most bizarre tale to tell of all these great grounds. It concerns the rugby match played between Wales and England on January 8, 1887 – the first 'international' to be staged at Llanelli. Preparations had been gathering steam for weeks and the excitement was growing daily. In fact, the match was the main topic of conversation both in the town and beyond.

4

However, things did not go quite to plan. The weather in the days leading up to the match had been bitterly cold and the first light of dawn on that Saturday morning showed that almost one half of the playing surface was frozen solid. It came as no surprise therefore that when the England captain, Alan Rotherham, came to inspect the pitch, he was unwilling to proceed as conditions were far too dangerous. For their part, the Welsh officials were keen to stage the encounter and assured everyone that by the afternoon's kick-off time all would be well. The weather forecasters had, after all, predicted a sunny day!

In today's vocabulary the words 'stress' and 'pressure of work' are as commonplace as currants in a fruit cake, but in 1887 they seem unlikely buzz words. However, can you imagine the stress and pressure that was put on the poor groundsman to get the field ready for the match? After all, some 8,000 tickets had been sold and it was reasonable to assume that some two thirds of these ticket holders were already on their way to Llanelli. If these people turned up only to be told that the match was cancelled . . . well, the consequences would be disastrous, riotous even! It is also fair to say that as far back as 1887, the Welsh Rugby Union officials were mindful of the revenue such an event generated and the prospect of having to refund money was not an option. To say that a heated debate went on behind the scenes is to understate the potential explosiveness of the situation.

As is often the case, help came from the most unexpected source. The Reverend Charles Newman (who was captain of Newport and Wales) had taken a stroll to the neighbouring cricket field while he mulled over the serious issues under discussion. Now with no stand to shelter the playing surface from the sun, the cricket outfield had thawed considerably and was in relatively good condition: firm but playable. After a brief consultation with his counterpart, it was decided that the game would indeed take place – albeit on the cricket ground and not the rugby pitch!

While this was good news for the most part, there were those present who objected and were most unhappy with the situation. Had they not paid to sit in the temporary stands and watch the match in comfort? There were no such elevated positions on the adjacent ground and every one would have to stand around the sidelines to view the proceedings. Now, if they were lucky they might catch a glimpse of a red or a white shirt when the play was near their end, or mark the trajectory of a brown-leather object against a pewter-coloured sky. It was hardly what these people had hoped for in an international match but that is exactly what happened.

The game went ahead and the vast majority present declared the event a huge success, so much so that the sports writers in the Monday editions of their newspapers wrote, 'A crowd of 8,000 saw a brilliant game, played 40 minutes each way despite the hard ground and the snow and sleet which fell in the second half.'

And what of the game itself? Would Wales again adopt the same approach as that which had cost them dearly in the match against Scotland the previous year? For that encounter, captain Frank Hancock of Cardiff had fielded the same formation that had proved so successful for his club, employing seven forwards and four centre three-quarters. That afternoon, however, the seven Welsh forwards were no match for the Scottish eight and Wales lost the match by two goals and a try to nil. It is interesting to note that an agreed basic formula for the balance of a team was not reached until the early part of the last century. Indeed one could easily write a tome to rival Tolstoy's *War and Peace* on the different formations employed by those early rugby teams – but that will have to wait for another day!

To return to the match at Stradey in 1887 . . . It was agreed that the team would feature three three-quarters. This decision was reached after a great deal of debate, the committee having heard a strong case brought by Arthur ('Monkey') Gould and seconded by the Reverend Charles Newman. Now Arthur Joseph Gould was considered something of a superstar in his playing days, the David Beckham of his era. The nickname 'Monkey' was adopted while he was still a young lad at school and came from the fact that he was always climbing trees. Indeed it was said many years later that had Gould been at his peak in the Thirties then maybe he and not Johnny Weismuller would have won the role of Tarzan on the big screen!

Be that as it may, Arthur Gould's climbing skills were brought into use on that January afternoon when the makeshift wooden crossbar became dislodged from the uprights and the rubber-like Gould shimmied up the posts to restore

Players of the period.

6

matters! As if this feat was not enough, he also came close to scoring the winning goal for Wales. Unfortunately, the ball missed the far post by inches and the result was a scoreless draw.

When the final whistle was blown, the crowd that made its way from Stradey was not wholly dissatisfied. At least they had not lost – the forwards had battled bravely but the backs had not proved adventurous enough and had relied too much on the kicking game rather than passing the ball along the line. During phases of play when the ball went loose, the English players proved dominant, a fact which was not lost on the Stradey faithful with their inherent understanding of the game!

It is interesting to note that the only Llanelli representative in the Wales XV on January 8, 1887 was Harry Bowen – an idol at Stradey ever since his first appearance for them at fifteen years of age. This truly was a unique day in the annals of rugby history when the first international at Stradey Park was played, not on the rugby pitch, but on the adjoining cricket field!

3

Llanelli 3   New Zealand Maoris 0

Harry Bowen's remarkable drop goal in 1888.

Much is made these days of the sacrifices made by sportsmen and women who abandon their families and friends to pursue their objectives. Imagine therefore the reaction of the New Zealand farmer's wife whose husband, on arriving home after a busy day tending the sheep, announced that he would be away for a while playing rugby, touring New Zealand, Australia and Great Britain. Oh! . . . and did he mention that he would be away for a total of fourteen months!

This new concept of a 'tour' had begun in early 1888 when a Great Britain side had ventured to the other side of the world to play games in Australia and New Zealand. Unfortunately the team lost its captain early on in the tour when R.L. Seddon drowned in a rowing accident in Australia.

From a playing perspective, however, the tour was an unbridled success. Never before had a team played with such abandon and creativity. Rugby, as it was played in New Zealand at that time, relied heavily on forward strength and domination with little emphasis on back play. So the New Zealand fullback, Joe Warbrick, hugely impressed by the style of play of the visitors, decided to arrange a return visit to the British Isles. He felt strongly that New Zealand rugby could only benefit from this new learning experience.

Joe was one of three brothers chosen to represent the New Zealand Maoris in this new venture, one of whom, William, is to this day regarded as one of the finest, most flamboyant backs ever to play for New Zealand. During this time the team played a total of 107 games, three of which were contested within the space of three days, and 78 of which they won!

The match staged at Stradey Park on December 19, 1888 was the first the visitors played in Wales and three thousand of the Llanelli faithful came to support their team. It was a cold, bright, sunny day and the pitch was in perfect condition for the match. The teams received a warm welcome as they ran out onto the field but this soon gave way to curiosity and a certain amount of unease as the Maoris performed their, by now, familiar Haka, challenging the opposition with their war-like movements and chanting *'Ake, Ake, Kia, Kaha'*. This, loosely translated, means 'brave, confident and adventurous'.

Modern methods of travel have evolved to such an extent that it is difficult for us in the twenty-first century to appreciate how difficult it was in those days to stage such an event. The journey taken by ship from the Antipodes took months in itself. The usual mode of transport, once they had arrived in Britain, was train, this being the era before Benz and Daimler had developed

Harry Bowen and his wife, Annie.

the motor car. Thus it was that the team arrived at Swansea and transferred to their headquarters at the Mackworth Hotel situated on the High Steeet, close to the railway station. Once the premier hotel in the city, the Mackworth was demolished in the 1950s.

Even if motorised transport had been available in 1888, it is difficult to imagine how travellers would have negotiated the highways. While the streets in town were mostly cobbled, the country roads were nothing short of dirt tracks and full of potholes (sounds familiar!). Therefore, for the last stage of the journey, we can only assume that the players again took the train from Swansea to Llanelli and then walked the remaining distance to Stradey Park. Here they would play their part in creating history as the first overseas team to play on the ground.

So much for the background. What of the game itself? The Llanelli captain, D.R. Williams, called correctly and chose to play 'up the hill' in the first half – an ill-advised decision according to those 'experts' in the crowd. There was very little to separate the two teams in the opening exchanges. The visitors were fired up with enthusiasm and keen to show their expertise. Llanelli, however, were equal to the task, defended well where necessary and were physically on a par with their opponents.

The Maoris' captain, Joe Warbrick, proved an elusive runner and on several occasions came close to scoring a try. Equally impressive was the visitors' scrummaging technique, their tight binding and low body positions producing a powerful, concerted shove. Their attacking edge was, however, blunted when the penetrative Henry Wynyard was well and truly thumped by some of the Llanelli forwards. Although he decided to continue playing, the scars, both emotional and physical, had the desired effect and it was a much more subdued Wynyard who completed the game.

As the minutes ticked by, Llanelli grew in confidence and it took a supreme effort by Joe Warbrick to chase and fall bravely onto the bouncing ball near his own line to save a certain try. This after a magnificent display of running and dribbling by D.J. Daniels, Gitto Griffiths and Dai Jones, any one of whom could had scored.

The vital score, the ultimate match-winner, came in the dying minutes of the first half. A long kick from Tom Morgan sailed over the try-line and had to be hastily grounded by one of the New Zealand players. From the resulting drop-out, the ball went directly to the Llanelli centre three-quarter, Harry Bowen, who was positioned on the halfway line. In an instant he surveyed the scene, adjusted his equilibrium and then fired the heavy leather ball towards the goal posts. What had hitherto been an extremely lively and vociferous crowd suddenly fell silent and watched incredulously as the ball sailed through the air and straight between the uprights. The resulting noise was unbelievable because in those days a drop goal was equivalent to three tries! Surely a winning score?

When everyone had resettled after the interval, it was obvious that the visitors weren't going to yield without a fight. As *The Western Mail* said: 'The game in the second half was exceedingly fast, and the ball was rushed about the field at great speed.' Time and again the Scarlets had to tackle bravely within inches of their try-line but the home team's defence stood firm and no one was more prominent than Harry Bowen himself who launched himself at the opposition on numerous occasions.

The pressure during the final few minutes was intense: Joe Warbrick was in the act of scoring when Harry Bowen's text-book tackle upended him, dislodging the ball. With only seconds remaining, Bowen was again in the thick of the action, sprinting and diving desperately to charge down Wynyard's attempt to level the score with a kick from a mark.

When the game ended, the reaction of the crowd was that of pure ecstasy – all fifteen players were hailed as heroes and borne from the field of play on the shoulders of their adoring fans. The final word comes from *Old Stager* in *The Western Mail*:

> The kick was a scorcher, the ball being propelled over the bar from half distance. The spectators, and even the Maoris, cheered this lustily – as well they might, for a better kick was never brought off on a football field.

There have, over the years, been many drop kicks at goal which have resulted in spectacular victories. As well as Jonny Wilkinson's effort against Australia in the World Cup Final in 2003, who can forget Joel Stransky's extra-time strike which brought delight to Nelson Mandela and the entire Rainbow Nation in 1995? Some will remember that the Dax and France outside half, Pierre Albaladejo, was the first to succeed with three drop goals in an international against Ireland at Stade Colombes in 1960; others that Jannie de Beer dropped five goals against England in the 1999 World Cup Quarter Finals. And what of Rob Andrew's last-minute effort which defeated Australia at Newlands, Cape Town in the 1995 World Cup Quarter Final? Or Jeremy Guscott's cheeky attempt in Durban in 1997 which resulted in a Lions' series win? And of course we mustn't forget our own local hero from Cefneithin; Barry John, supplying the *coup de grâce* for Cardiff with four drop goals against Llanelli in 1968. These players' names have all been entered into the history books and recorded for posterity but we cannot forget that game in 1888 when Harry Bowen scored the winning points for Llanelli against the New Zealand Maoris – what a game and what a kick!

4

Who Beat the Wallabies?

Yes . . . the old Sosban Fach, and Tom the driving force.

How does one go about choosing the best prop forward to have represented Llanelli Rugby Football Club? The task is not an easy one – Emrys Evans (who played in the front and back row for Wales), Griff Bevan, Henry Morgan, Howard 'Ash' Davies, Byron Gale, John Warlow, Tony Crocker, Laurance Delaney, Ricky Evans are all names that immediately spring to mind. Each of these would bring his own special quality to the role and each would merit an entire chapter in another volume.

However, if forced to choose one name to be pencilled in alongside those of Barry Llewellyn and Norman Gale in the front row of my Llanelli Dream Team, I would plump for Tom Evans. Born and brought up in Ammanford in the Amman Valley, Tom Evans won 18 caps for Wales in the early part of the twentieth century. Indeed, he must have made quite an impression on the Welsh Selection Committee of the day as it was highly unusual for anyone who lived or played to the west of the Loughor Bridge to be included in the national XV.

Rugby articles written during that period show that he was regarded as one of the best players of his day. As strong as an ox and full of stamina, he was also unusally fleet of foot. This was a great advantage in those days as the laws then allowed the first player to reach a scrummage to form the front row.

It was Tom (who was by now captain of Llanelli) who scored the winning try for his club against Australia in 1908, crossing the try-line with three Wallabies clinging on to his muscular frame. And it is to that 8-3 victory that the famous extra verse to 'Sosban Fach' refers.

The match report in the *Llanelly and County Guardian* read:

> With honours equally divided, the Scarlets showed that they still meant business by again invading the vistors' territory. It was Llanelly's ball, about fifteen yards from the line, and Tom Evans, running at full tilt, took the ball with a safe pair of hands, and in the next instant was over the line without having been thrown out of his stride. It was a geat try, and a fitting reward to the brilliant game which Evans played. He is undoubtedly the best forward in Wales today.

Tom and the team that beat the Wallabies on October 12, 1908.

Back row (left to right): T.R. Mills (chairman), Jim Watts, Jack Auckland, D. Llewellyn Bowen, A.J. Stacey, Will Cole, Ike Lewis, W.J. (Fishguard) Thomas, Tom Miller (committee member).

Middle row (left to right): Handel Richards, Y Parch. Tom Williams, Tom Evans (captain), Harvey Thomas, Will Thomas.

Front row (left to right): Dai Lloyd, Harry Morgan, Willie Arnold, W.H. Davies (Mabon), spongeman.

5

The Terrible Eight

The Reverend Alban Davies's angels!

The Infamous Terrible Eight!.
Back row (left to right): Percy Llewellyn Jones (Pontypool),
Edgar Morgan (Swansea), Harry Uzzell (Newport), Thomas John Lloyd (Neath),
David Watts (Maesteg).
Front row (left to right): Tom Williams (Swansea), The Revd Jenkin Alban Davies (Llanelli),
Walter Rees (WRU secretary), John 'Bedwellty' Jones (Abertillery).

To the list 'The Famous Five' and 'The Secret Seven' can be added 'The Terrible Eight'. But these were no harmlessly adventurous school-book characters. They were, rather, the Wales pack of forwards, led by the Reverend Alban Davies, whose exploits had already won one Grand Slam for their team and who brought them within a whisker of a second one in the last year of peace before the outbreak of the Great War.

In his later years the Reverend Davies was asked by one commentator how was it that a man of the cloth was able to tolerate the colourful language heard in the set scrummage? The reply was that the skull cap which he wore served more than one purpose!

It is interesting to note that several clergymen represented Wales at rugby during the latter stages of the nineteenth and the beginning of the twentieth century. Historians maintain that this was as a result of the missionary work carried out at that time in the industrial valleys of Wales. There was also a strong connection between the Roman Catholic Church and the development of rugby clubs in the Cardiff and Port Talbot areas of South Wales. Further afield it could be seen that Everton, Wolverhampton Wanderers, Aston Villa and Bolton Wanderers football clubs originated from their early connection with the church.

The Welsh rugby team of 1881 boasted three Anglican churchmen – the captain, James Alfred Bevan, who hailed from Abergavenny; Charles Newman from Newport and Edward Peake, a native of Chepstow. After the Great War, W.T. Havard, born and brought up in Llanelli, played for Wales against a New Zealand Army XV. He went on to become Bishop of St Asaph and St David's.

But to return to the 1913/14 international season and to the match against England at Twickenham . . . As is often the case in these encounters, Wales were the better team and played the more stylish rugby but lost the match. With two minutes of the game remaining, Wales were ahead by nine points to five thanks to a try by the Llanelli centre three-quarter Willie Watts and a mighty drop goal from the boot of George Hirst, the Newport wing. Seconds later the hero Watts became the villain of the piece as he dropped a straightforward pass close to his try-line. This allowed the England wing forward and renowned poacher 'Cherry' Spillman to score an effortless try which was converted by Fred Taylor. Thus it was that at the final whistle it was the men in white who were celebrating an undeserved victory.

Three weeks later, Wales were hosts to Scotland at Cardiff and secured victory in front of a respectable crowd of 35,000 people. It is interesting to note that the Llanelli three-quarter, Ivor Davies, scored a try on his first appearance in a Welsh jersey. The Welsh forwards were the heroes of the hour, but the whole event was overshadowed by comments made by the Scottish captain, Davis McLaren Bain, in his after-dinner speech. Conceding defeat he said that the 'dirtiest team had won on the day'. Andrew 'Jock' Wemyss won his first cap for Scotland in this match. In later years he was a distinguished writer and broadcaster on rugby football and one of the committee members of the Barbarians club. Despite losing an eye in the war, he continued playing for Scotland in the 1920s, along with many others of the 1914 team.

The third encounter in the series was played on March 2, against France at St Helen's in Swansea. The score was 31-0 in favour of Wales – the Reverend Alban Davies scoring one of seven tries. Five of these efforts were converted by Jack Bancroft.

The final match took place at Balmoral Park in Belfast. The press reports described the contest as being 'physical and unpleasant' – indeed many went on to describe it as the dirtiest encounter to date. It was after this that the Welsh pack were named 'The Terrible Eight'. Mind you, by all accounts, the Irish forwards were themselves no angels and gave as good as they got in most quarters. Even though the result showed a win for Wales, the Irish followers felt it was their men who had won the battle.

The bad feeling between the two sides had begun long before kick-off. On the eve of the match, the Irish squad had marched into the visitors' hotel and publicly humiliated and taunted the Welsh players with verbal threats. Their ringleader was the pack leader, Dr William Tyrell, who singled out the Pontypool forward Percy Jones (himself a muscular miner) and warned him that he would be leaving the field of play blacker than he emerged from the coalface. Jones's response was to smile at his taunter and shrug his shoulders.

The following afternoon, once the game was under way, the Irish players carried out their threats and took the law into their own hands. At times it seemed as if the spectators were witnessing a crowd scene from a Western film where the villain enters the saloon and all hell breaks loose. It certainly required John Wayne to referee the match! There was no respect for the laws of the game and indeed a firmer referee would have sent at least six players from the field of play. As it was, the Scottish official, Mr Tulloch, turned a blind eye to proceedings and the 'game' continued.

Wales were again victorious (in both aspects of the encounter) with tries being scored by Bedwellty Jones (Abertillery), Ivor Davies (Llanelli) and Jack Wetter (Newport). In the after-match pleasantries, Dr Tyrrell is reported to have singled out Percy Jones and acknowledged him with the words 'You're the only Welshman who ever beat me.'

In a postscript to the drama it was years later that two former internationals were sitting side by side in the North Stand at Cardiff Arms Park. They were reminiscing about the years that had gone by, while at the same time acknowledging the feats of Jackie Kyle and Cliff Morgan on the playing field. The year was 1951 and the two former players were Percy Jones (the former miner) and Dr W.M. Tyrrell (the President of the Irish Rugby Union).

The Reverend Alban Davies passed away in 1976 at the grand old age of ninety. He had settled in San Francisco during his later years. The two old friends, Tyrrell and Jones, died within six months of each other in 1969 when both were 82 years old. Whatever the history books tell us, I can assure you that World War One started on March 14, 1914 at Balmoral Park in Belfast!

6

Albert

Only the unconverted could ask 'Albert who?'

To Victoria, Queen of England and Empress of India, Albert was the light of her life, her dear husband and soulmate. Add Einstein to the Christian name and there is a man revered by mathematicians and scientists the world over. To the musicians and philosophers of the world, there is only one Albert – Albert Schweitzer. To those film buffs amongst us, the name Albert can only be followed by the surname 'Finney'.

Yet if one were to mention the name to the Llanelli faithful, only one Albert would spring to mind: Albert Jenkins, the charismatic, multi-talented centre three-quarter who played for Llanelli and Wales in the period following the First World War. He was a giant of a man in every sense of the word. Almost six feet tall, weighing thirteen stone, possessing huge shoulders and a muscular chest, Albert Jenkins was a steelworker by profession. This was a gruelling occupation by any standards, especially so during the early part of the twentieth century. The hours were long. A typical shift would last for twelve hours, whether this was from 6am to 6pm or vice versa, which left no time for any recreational activities. Indeed, most men went home so exhausted that after their meal they would just collapse into their beds.

Added to the fact that the working hours were long, it was also necessary to spend a great deal of time outdoors, unloading consignments of iron ore as they arrived at the North Dock in Llanelli. During the winter months the weather conditions could be unrelenting with cold, driving rain and biting winds taking their toll on all but the most hardy of individuals. It was no surprise, therefore, that a large number of workmen went to an early grave.

Given that these were the working conditions prevalent in the area during this time, it is a miracle that any young man had either the inclination or the stamina to take part in any sporting activities. That he did take part and succeed at the highest level says much about the strength of character and physical prowess of Albert Jenkins. It was not considered unusual to see Albert (and many of his contemporaries also) arrive at Stradey Park straight from the furnaces. With muddied faces they would be bathed in perspiration and often hungry (from lack of food in many instances) for the battle ahead. For these young men, the eighty or so minutes they spent running around a rugby field was a welcome release from the rigours of day-to-day life.

The supporters at Stradey Park appreciated the sacrifices that these young men made, so when one of them, in the shape of Albert, produced such electrifying performances on a Saturday afternoon, he was hailed as a

Albert Jenkins in his Welsh shirt and cap.

superstar. A few years ago, I had the enjoyable privilege of spending an afternoon in the company of Rees Thomas, a former Llanelli wing forward. At that time Rees was 98 years of age but could vividly recall his playing days at Stradey Park. His hero was undoubtedly Albert Jenkins and the following words are Rees's own tribute to the great man, translated from his first language, Welsh.

When I arrived home from work, I saw that someone had conveniently left a copy of the *Llanelly Mercury* on the kitchen table. However, before I had time to pick up and read the newspaper the family rushed in and announced the good news. Llanelli were about to embark on a tour of Cornwall over the Easter holidays and I had been chosen to represent the Scarlets. This was a dream come true because in those days every boy in the area wanted to play for Llanelli. But for me there was also something else – I would be playing in the same team as Albert.

If Albert were alive today he would be a millionaire – he was a genius, a real superstar. He was a big man, his two hands were like spades, that came from his job as a loader in the North Dock. You should see the way he handled bags of potatoes – anyone would think they were bags of crisps! As well as being powerful, Albert was also quick, especially over the first ten yards and he could kick the ball. He was as good as George Nepia, which is praise indeed!

He could also read the game astutely, pick out the weaknesses in the opposition and if some youngster was unfortunate enough to be playing at full back – look out! Despite all the attention he received, Albert Jenkins was a quiet man. I remember one incident when we played at Newport and after the match we had to attend a dinner at the town's Westgate Hotel. All the important people of the town were there and as team captain, Albert was asked to say a few words. When his turn came, he was nowhere to be seen – he had crept out of the room by crawling under the tables!

Albert Jenkins was truly a heroic figure in Llanelli. It wasn't unusual to see a large queue of fans standing patiently hours before a match just to catch a glimpse of him as he arrived or to offer to carry his bag when he left after the game. Such was his drawing power that if, by some quirk of fate, Albert could not take to the field because of injury or work commitment, the fans would leave the stadium in droves and not bother to watch the ensuing match.

Albert, however, did have his critics. There were those who maintained that his best playing days were reserved for Stradey Park and that his performances in the national team were below par. That he played just fourteen games for Wales during his career was a disgrace. As was to happen so many times in the years that followed, the Welsh selectors were only interested in choosing players from clubs east of the Loughor Bridge.

Albert had many qualities but his most outstanding one I believe was his ability to change the course of a match. In this respect he was in a class of his own. The first occasion Albert appeared in the scarlet jersey of Llanelli was against Neath at the Gnoll. Although the visitors lost the match by eight points to nil, the travelling supporters were given a foretaste of what was to come when Jenkins produced one electrifying run of some fifty yards.

Encouraged by what they had seen against Neath, the Llanelli diehards turned up in their thousands to witness their new star produce one superb performance after another. Indeed so great were the crowds thereafter that Llanelli RFC was able to clear its outstanding debts to creditors by the end of the season.

At the end of the 1918/19 season the following piece appeared in the *Evening Post*:

> There is a rugby footballer at Llanelly called Albert Jenkins. He is a tinplater by trade, and in his spare time, since he returned from France a few weeks ago, after long service, he wins matches for Llanelly by kicking goals and scoring no end of tries. The bigger the match, the better he performs. He is worshipped by the Llanelly crowd, half of whom are attracted week by week simply to see Jenkins display his skill. He is as good as Rhys Gabe at his very best, and everybody who has seen him play knows this, except the Welsh Football Union. But news travels fast, and there is a more active body in control of the Northern Union. They have heard of Jenkins's ability and attempted to get his signature long ago without success. They are determined to get Jenkins. One Northern Union player said they were going to get Jenkins, whatever his price. The news of the offer soon got about Llanelly and a warm reception was threatened for any Northern Union men who offer Jenkins further inducements to go North, and a local boxer (Billy Roberts) is said to be keeping a watchful eye for any strangers in the camp.

The 1920 international season saw Albert again make his mark in the Welsh jersey. Against Ireland he contributed a drop goal, kicked two conversions, scored a try whilst also creating three scoring opportunities for Bryn Williams. A year later against Scotland he destroyed the defensive line, but his fellow three-quarters were unable to capitalise on his efforts. His opponents complained bitterly that he was an extremely difficult player to tackle as he was so physically strong but at the same time fleet of foot. Others were caught out by the fact that they couldn't predict whether he was going to run, pass or kick. Everything he did was instinctive and this made him an impossible player to read.

The 1927/28 season saw Llanelli win the unofficial club championship in Wales. This forced the Welsh selectors to choose six players from the side to be included in the international team. Thus Albert Jenkins was restored to the international arena after being overlooked for four seasons. His recall prompted an unexpected win at Murrayfield against Scotland.

Albert played his last international match for Wales against Ireland at Cardiff on March 10, 1928. 'Scrap the lot' was the chant from the terraces as the team lost by 13 points to 10 and this despite a valiant effort from Albert who scored one try and Dai John a second. Five more seasons would pass before he decided to retire from playing rugby for Llanelli. By now he was accorded god-like status by the Scarlet supporters and to this day his type of play is regarded as a benchmark against which all centre three-quarters are measured.

Albert Jenkins passed away in October 1953 – he was 58 years old. Thousands of people lined the streets as the cortège, which included the town's civic dignitaries, passed by. It was a fitting farewell to one who many people regard as one of the finest rugby players that Llanelli and Wales have produced.

Llanelli, 1920-21.
Back row (left to right): Ben James, David Williams, Howard Hughes, Billy Lewis, Frank Evans.
Standing: D. Hopkin Thomas, George Morgan, Gwyn Francis, Revd J. G. Stephens, Edgar Morgan, Aneurin Thomas, Gethin Thomas, W.J. Jones, W.J. (Fishguard) Thomas.
Seated: E.E. Bailey (secretary), Fred Samuel, 'Hendy' Evans, Idwal Thomas, Bryn S. Evans (captain), D. Pearson (president), Albert Jenkins, Emlyn Morgan, Oswald Morgan (chairman).
Front row: Sid Congdon, T.J. Bowen, 'Billo' Rees, W.H. Davies ('Mabon')

(Photo presented to Llanelli RFC by Misses Ray and Val J. R. Thomas, Llwynhendy.)

7

Jac Elwyn

The wronged winger

Jac Elwyn Evans was my grandmother's brother. Another of his sisters was the great-grandmother of one of the most exciting players of the modern era, Shane Williams.

Jac Elwyn was born in Lower Brynaman in the Amman Valley, that part of the village located in Glamorgan (or currently Neath/Port Talbot) as opposed to Upper Brynaman which is still in Carmarthenshire. By day, Jac Elwyn was a miner, as were most of the young men who lived in the South Wales valleys at that time. Life was physically hard – indeed in that period the muscular bodies of the rugby players were acquired from their day-to-day tasks at the coalface not, as is the norm today, from endless hours spent in the gym!

However, as in the present professional structure, being able to run onto a rugby field on a Saturday afternoon needed the support of a back-up team and in Jac Elwyn's case that team was his understanding wife, Nansi, and the very accommodating manager of the colliery where he was an employee.

Jac Elwyn Evans represented the Scarlets in the Twenties of the last century. He was a prolific try-scorer, with 17 tries to his name during the 1922/23 season and 23 tries the following year. He was also to figure prominently in the games versus the New Zealand All Blacks and the New Zealand Maoris. The Welsh selectors could not ignore such performances and as a result he was selected to play for Wales against Scotland at Inverleith in Edinburgh on February 2, 1924. Two of his Llanelli team-mates were also to play in that match, namely the wing forward Ivor Jones and Gwyn Francis who played at No 8.

Unfortunately, it was not a game that one of the trio would care to remember. Wales were well and truly trounced by the Scots, who ran in eight tries compared to the two claimed by Jack Whitfield's team. The Welsh forwards were no match for their counterparts and as a result the Scottish backs were given free rein to exhibit their skills. The four three-quarters involved that afternoon, Ian Smith, Phil McPherson, George Aitken and Johnnie Wallace, were all undergraduates at Oxford University and were well used to playing together on a regular basis.

Ian Smith, in particular, was a human dynamo, scoring 24 tries in 32 appearances on the wing for Scotland. Indeed until recently he held the record for the most tries scored for his country. It is hardly surprising therefore that he was known as 'The Flying Scotsman'. Unfortunately for Wales, three of those 24 tries were scored on that day at Inverleith, a day when Wales suffered their heaviest defeat of the twentieth century and Jac Elwyn was part of that team!

Suffice it to say that the Llanelli flyer was not marking Ian Smith on that fateful day, his opponent being Johnnie Wallace, who did not score. At least some family pride remained intact! In the after-match dinner, Ian Smith was introduced to the hapless Harold Davies, the Newport wing three-quarter, who had been his opposite number in the Welsh team. Davies's remark broke the ice: ' I wondered who you were as I didn't see you all afternoon!'

Some fans were able to make the journey north to support their team. According to one, namely Teddy James, who had gone to support his brother-in-law from Brynaman, they were far outnumbered by the committee. In those days the only means of travel was by train and the cost of £1.30s compares favourably with the prices offered today by Ryanair and Easy Jet!

The morning after the match saw the entire Welsh squad make their biennial pilgrimage to Queensferry to view the famous bridge crossing the Firth of Forth; a bridge immortalised in the classic film *The Thirty-nine Steps*. This bridge was, and still is, a feat of engineering and architectural beauty and the story goes that as soon as painting work is complete it is time to start all over again! Be that as it may, it was a very subdued and down-hearted group of players who arrived on the banks of the Forth that cold February morning. Their misery was compounded when one of the Welsh Rugby Union committeemen was heard to mutter, 'Enjoy the spectacle boys. This is the last

Wronged? Yes, but the supporters worshipped him!

time you'll see this, courtesy of the WRU.' Unfortunately, in the case of Jac Elwyn Evans and several of the others, this proved to be true but to her dying day, my grandmother maintained that Jac Elwyn had been hard done by!

It was during his last season at Llanelli that Jac Elwyn played a match against his old club Amman United. The date was September 13, 1925. If the match had been played on Friday the Thirteenth, the ensuing events could not have been more bizarre. The game itself was well contested and played in the best spirit of rugby football. However, the first half was interrupted for ten minutes when four Friesian cows strolled onto the pitch from a neighbouring field. In the dying minutes of the second half with neither side having scored, the referee had to call proceedings to an end. The river Aman, which runs alongside the playing area, was rising at an alarming rate in the heavy rain and the last remaining rugby ball was carried away by the strong current. The cry 'no-ball' is heard often enough during a cricket match but on that afternoon it was also heard loud and clear on the Amman United Rugby ground!

After his retirement from the game, Jac Elwyn and Nansi moved to live in Landore on the outskirts of Swansea where they ran a Workingmen's Club. It is still a sore point in the family: Jac Elwyn was shabbily treated by the WRU!

The Welsh team visit the Forth Bridge.   *Photograph by D. Thomas*

8

Ernie Finch's moment of glory

Good fortune or pure sorcery?

One of the most famous, or to some, infamous, soccer players of the modern era is the Argentinian striker Diego Maradona. While there are thousands of football fans who have witnessed first hand his amazing skills with the round ball, from the terraces at Napoli to the sponsors' boxes at Barcelona, the majority of us have only been able to sit in wonder in front of our television sets.

While the creativity of one genius, John Logie Baird, enabled us to appreciate the ingenuity of another, in the form of Maradona, the Sony and Toshiba era has also enabled everyone to remember one notorious incident above all others. It took place during the World Cup Finals in Mexico in 1986 when Argentina was playing England. 'The gods were smiling on him' was one of the newspaper headlines on the morning after the match. But this is not how the watching millions saw things. What most people witnessed was Maradona leaping into the air and using his arm to guide the ball into Peter Shilton's goal. That he scored again a few minutes later with a run which completely mesmerised the opposing English defence was of no consequence. Maradona had cheated and that event is forever etched on everyone's memory. One outrage by which an entire career is remembered.

And so it was with Ernie Finch. Finch played rugby for Llanelli during the 1920s, joining the Scarlets after several impressive performances for Pembroke Dock Quins. He scored 17 tries in 17 matches during his first season at Stradey Park and soon became a favourite with the supporters. In fact it is fair to say that if Albert Jenkins was the Phil Bennett of his day then Ernie Finch was its Ieuan Evans.

Honours with the national side soon followed as Ernie went on to win seven caps – three of these were against France against whom he again scored. The pinnacle of his career, however, came with the match against Cliff Porter's All Blacks on December 29, 1924. The game was staged at St Helen's in Swansea and records show the attendance to have been in the region of 50,000 people. There were three Llanelli players in the Welsh team that day: Ernie Finch, Albert Jenkins and the forward Cliff Williams. The visitors were determined to avenge their defeat in Cardiff twenty years earlier and that is exactly what happened. But to quote Napoleon Bonaparte, 'Not victory, annihilation.' The final score read Wales 0 New Zealand 19. As the supporters filed away despondently from the ground, all they could do was recognise the fact that the home team had been outclassed and outgunned in all phases of play.

The hero of the afternoon was the nineteen-year-old fullback George Nepia. He seemed to be everywhere on the field. If one of the Welsh forwards broke through the defence and started on a charge, Nepia would be there with a crunching tackle. On more than one occasion he would fall onto a loose ball, spring back upright and then produce a kick of some distance all in one movement. All Albert and Ernie could do was stand and stare in admiration.

However, Ernie's big moment came four days later when New Zealand travelled to West Wales to play Llanelli. Thanks to the enterprising Llanelli committee of the day, the ground had been transformed into an international arena. Temporary stands had been erected all around Stradey Park, the roads leading to the venue had been cleared and most of the match tickets had been sold weeks in advance.

The Monday before the encounter saw the announcement of the New Zealand team. Some commentators were heard to declare that this side was a more powerful one than that which had beaten Wales at St Helen's! Of course, this was a great compliment to the Llanelli side and such was the anticipation that the crowds started arriving at eleven o'clock on the morning of the match.

Llanelli chose to field eight forwards while the All Blacks kept to their normal pattern of seven. From the first whistle the home side played like men possessed. But despite an exceptionally fast, exciting and well-contested half, the Scarlets found themselves trailing by eight points to nil after 25 minutes play, Hart and Svenson scoring a try apiece for the visitors with Nepia adding a conversion.

During this era, and indeed up until the 1970s, it was the wing three-quarter who would throw the ball into the lines-out. And so it was that, just before half-time, Ernie Finch found himself aiming the ball at the two second-row forwards, Gwyn Francis and Willie Lewis. Now this move had been rehearsed on countless occasions during practice sessions but would it work against the mighty All Blacks?

Fortunately, that afternoon all the Llanelli players were operating on the same wavelength and no sooner had the ball been thrown into the line-out than it returned like a bullet into the waiting hands of Ernie. He immediately took off like a greyhound released from its trap and sprinted for the New Zealand try-line. The All Black defence was completely wrong-footed and there was only one player standing between Ernie Finch and immortality. He was, of course, none other than George Nepia.

What happened next is a part of Llanelli folklore. While he was only yards from glory and an arm's length away from the greatest fullback in world rugby, Finch suddenly stopped dead in his tracks. Whether it was sheer panic on his part or a stroke of genius only he would ever know. At any rate, the fullback had already launched himself in the direction of the Llanelli wing three-quarter with a tackle which, had it been successful, would undoubtedly have resulted in Finch being stretchered off the field. However, Nepia found himself clutching at air. Meanwhile, Finch regained his momentum and composure and scrambled over the try-line for a splendid score.

When the final whistle blew, the visitors had scored eight points to Llanelli's three. The New Zealand All Blacks went on to win every one of their games on that tour of 1924/25 but Cliff Porter and his team ranked that game on December 2, 1924, at Stradey Park as one of their most difficult.

Thus it is that as everyone associates Maradona with that one incident in Mexico City, then Ernie Finch's cameo at Stradey ensures his place in the annals of the history of Llanelli RFC. The final word goes to George Nepia:

> Rumours have been circling that when Ernie Finch scored he was so scared that he stopped dead in his tracks and that when I went through with my tackle, I missed him and that this was how he reached the try-line.
> The truth is that Ernie Finch broke through and that when I was getting across to tackle him, he showed what a brilliant winger he was. At the critical moment, and just a second or two before I launched the tackle, Ernie swerved into me, breaking my speed and my timing and then swung outwards again. By the time I regathered speed, Ernie had scored a lovely try.

Ernie Finch in his
Welsh shirt and cap

9

Ivor Jones

Mr 100%

Since its inception, Llanelli RFC (along with every other major rugby club) owes its success to numerous feeder clubs who provide opportunities for many up-and-coming players. Some take advantage and go on to become stars of the future. In the case of Llanelli, these clubs would include Llandybie, Ammanford, Hendy, Cwmllynfell, Gorseinon, Felinfoel, Loughor etc. Smaller village clubs became nursery units, nurturing the talents of young players and preparing them both physically and mentally for that step up to the higher echelons of the game.

It is interesting to note, however, that an invitation to play for a major club did not always merit an acceptance. For many young men, just to play for the village club was enough of a reward. After all, they were among friends. This was their social sphere and this is where they felt comfortable. They did not feel the need to spend a day travelling to some alien environment and they certainly weren't going to forfeit a shift's pay to accomplish this!

There is a humorous anecdote which encapsulates the era. During the late 1950s Cwmllynfell RFC was one of the foremost second-class sides in West Wales. This, after all, was where the late and great R.H. Williams embarked on his playing career. The team was at one time known locally as the 'Invincibles' as a result of one successful period in its history. They were held in high esteem and to be chosen for Cwmllynfell was to realise a childhood dream.

Thus it was that on a certain Saturday afternoon in October, the valley outfit made the journey to Fairwood on the outskirts of Swansea to play Swansea Uplands. The match resulted in an easy win for the visitors. It is not recorded how many of the Uplands' players were Welsh-speaking (most probably none) but all the Cwmllynfell XV spoke the language of heaven. The captain's instruction to the pack was *'Ar ei hôl hi!'* – roughly translated as 'After it!' (i.e after the ball). This was repeated time and again throughout the duration of the game. As a result the forwards swarmed around the field like bees and completely overwhelmed the opposition.

Now the referee that day was a gentleman by the name of George Llewellyn, who hailed from Brynaman. As was his custom on a Monday evening he picked up his copy of *The South Wales Evening Post* from the local newsagent. In those days it was usual to find snippets relating to games played in the West Wales League recorded in the sporting section. Imagine his reaction therefore when he read the following report:

Cwmllynfell owed their victory to the superb performance of their Italian born flanker Arioli who must surely be destined for international honours.

Ivor Jones did not play for Cwmllynfell – his club was Loughor which he represented in the early 1920s. By day he worked the furnaces at Bynea and at weekends he turned out for his local team. This was an era of extreme hardship. If an individual was to succeed, it meant making many sacrifices, whether this was on an economic or social level. The prevailing situation at the time demanded complete commitment if one was to rise above the abject poverty and mundanity of day-to-day life.

It was commitment and dedication which saw Cwmllynfell succeed at Fairwood and it was commitment which ran through the veins of every player at Loughor RFC, none more than Ivor Jones. Ivor played his first game for Llanelli on Boxing Day 1922 against London Welsh at Stradey Park. During the following season he scored 47 points which were made up of five tries, a drop goal, two penalties and eleven conversions. He went on to represent Birmingham, Wales and the British Lions in a career which spanned seventeen seasons. While touring New Zealand with the Lions in 1930, Ivor Jones was described in the local press as the best wing forward ever to have played in the islands. It was the red-headed forward's determination coupled with his natural talent that made such an impression on the All Blacks' journalists.

Llanelli 1935/36.
Back row (left to right): S.G.M. Jones (secretary), Gilbert Davies, Emrys Evans, Bryn Evans, Gwyn Monger, Percy Moxey, Arthur Every.
Middle row (left to right): Gwyn Treharne, Bill Clement, Reg Brown, Ivor Jones (captain), Graham Harries, Elvet Jones, Fred Morgan.
Front row (left to right): The Revd Jac Evans, The Revd Glyn Jones.

Terry McLean, the respected sports-writer, witnessed one of Ivor Jones's best ever performances in the First Test Match at Dunedin in 1930 and the following is his own account of that game:

We were down in their 25, I remember. Practically on the goal-line as a matter of fact. There wasn't more than a minute left for play. Porter put the ball in and we got it. I think Jimmy Mill was a bit off balance when he picked it up. It looked as if he might be going for one of those blind side tries of his. I suppose the way was blocked. That's when he turned and threw a pass at Herbie Lilburne.

It wasn't the best pass, but it looked good enough. It would have been good enough too, if it hadn't been for this bloody Welsh terror, Jones. He must have taken off from the side of the scrum like a shot, because he collected that pass at full speed. In a stride or two, he was clear of everybody. Amazing. I can still see him legging it up the field. Out towards the left touchline going up the Workshops end.

Of course, as you might expect, Cookie and Freddie Lucas started tearing back and George Nepia stood there like the Rock of Gibraltar, too. So things weren't as bad as they might have looked. Then this crafty Jones gives a bit of a dummy – no one but a Welshman would think of doing a thing like that – and our boys sat back on their hunkers for a moment.

And then Jones was on Nepia at halfway. You get the picture? Jones was here and Nepia was there. Out on the right was Cookie, going like a rocket. And on the left was this little bloke, Morley, close to touch and scampering. No one else mattered two hoots in hell. Except us. We were making enough noise to sink a ship.

Jones was practically in George's arms when he passed, so that cancelled George out. That left just two, Morley and Cooke. They had 50 yards to go. I'm telling you, they don't play football like it, these days. Fifty yards. Have you ever screamed so much you can't even hear yourself think? Have you ever picked your hat off and just let 'er go and be damned to all the colds that ever infested the earth? Have you ever just gone mad? With 27,000 others all doing the same thing?

If you haven't, you haven't lived. There they went. Fifty mortal yards. What a race! I'd die happy if I could see it again. The goal-line coming up and Cookie inching nearer and nearer. Almost ready to dive. And Morley zipping along. Immortal. Morley won by a yard.

And Britain won, by 6-3.

Cheering? I can hear it yet.

Despite having had such a successful Lions tour, Ivor Jones was ignored by the Welsh selectors. This remains a great mystery to this day. Or as the blare of the *Llanelly Mercury* would have it:

There was one selectorial decision that even struck many outside boiling Sospanville as bordering on lunacy.

The Big(-oted) Five – inexcusable insult to great Llanelly forward.

Having started his rugby career at fullback at Loughor, Ivor Jones then moved to play for Swansea for a short time before finally settling for Llanelli and playing regularly at Stradey Park. He was captain for nine seasons and led the Scarlets against the 1926 Maoris, 1927 Waratahs, 1931 Springboks and the 1935 All Blacks. As a player, apart from his obvious commitment to the game, he was also a very skilful dribbler of the ball and a creative runner at a time when such skills were not generally recognised (and not at all by the national selectors) in an open-side wing forward. He was constantly at hand to intimidate the opposing outside half and was ever present to pass on the scoring opportunities when they came.

As this was the 1920s and jobs were scarce, Ivor was forced to move his family to Birmingham to seek employment. Here he scored 34 tries for his new club. He played 522 games in the scarlet shirt of Llanelli, a record only recently passed in the 1990s by Phil May. When he finally retired from the game, Ivor became a successful administrator and became Chairman of the WRU during season 1968/69. He sadly passed away in 1982 at the age of 80.

Ivor crosses the try-line for Llanelli against the All Blacks in 1935. The try was disallowed!

10

Shamateurism

It seems that it was not Mohammed el Fayed, the millionaire businessman and owner of Harrods of Knightsbridge, who allegedly started the fashion of payment of moneys in plain brown envelopes. The broadcaster G.V. Wynne Jones wrote a book in the 1950s entitled *Shamateurism*. In the book he lists a whole number of prominent rugby players who were paid via such little envelopes. This payment came from a variety of sources, the most popular being the cash taken for car parking at grounds.

If one were to scan the car parks attached to rugby venues these days, then the wide variety of cars found there would do justice to many a West-End Garage. Be they BMWs, Audis, Porsches or the latest models of the top-of-the-range 4x4s, these are the vehicles that the modern-day rugby player is seen to drive. Add to this the Armani suits, the Gucci shoes, Oakley sunglasses and the Louis Vitton luggage and it is easy to see that these young sportsmen enjoy a jet-set lifestyle and command salaries large enough to support it.

This is true of many of the players at Llanelli – good luck to them. After all a rugby player's career is a relatively short one. If he escapes serious injury then the average length of time a player can command such a salary is around 12 years. This entails a strict code of self-discipline so that peak fitness and consistent performances on the field of play are the norm. If all these criteria are met, then the shrewd player will be able to invest wisely in order to support himself when his playing days are over. There will be those who can capitalise on their skills and transfer these to the business, administrative or broadcasting spheres.

How different things were in days of old! Before the First World War, to be paid a wage for playing rugby was unheard of. Men would earn their daily crust by sheer physical hard work whether this be at the coalface or in the glare of the furnace. It was not unusual to see these young men turn up for rugby training once or twice a week, with their bodies still soaked in sweat or their faces blackened with coal dust. Why did they do it? It was purely for the love of the game. When economic conditions became really desperate, hundreds left South Wales and migrated North, mostly to Lancashire and Yorkshire to play the professional game. This was their only means of employment and one which would ensure that they had a roof over their heads and a meal on the table.

Not that everyone agreed with this premiss. It was at Brynaman rugby club in the 1960s that I heard one member voice the opinion that one player of the era could not afford to go 'North' – he was too well paid at his present club! There is no evidence to suggest that this was true, or whether or not these payments were large or small, or took place on a regular basis. What is true to say is that in the first half of the last century the vast majority of rugby players weren't paid and in fact were themselves out of pocket as a result of commitments to the game. There may have been the odd reimbursement of ten shillings here or a pound there to make up for travelling expenses incurred but what is certain is that there was no payment in lieu if a player missed his shift at work. This would account for the exodus from the game by hordes of young men when strangers dressed in their Savile-Row suits came calling, brandishing their cheque books.

This mindset was not exclusive to club rugby. In fact, the ethos was even more jealously guarded in the international arena. It was impossible to fool the accountants at the WRU head office. They knew exactly the price of a return train ticket from Llanelli to Cardiff! If the Welsh financiers were thought to be thrifty, their English counterparts were even worse as the following anecdote illustrates. H. C. Catcheside (who scored six tries in his first four games for England) submitted his expenses after one game, claiming £3 for a ticket from Newcastle to London. The R.F.U. Treasurer contacted Euston Station, to be told that the tricket price was in fact £2.19s.11d (£2.99 in today's money). And this was the sum paid to Catcheside for his trouble.

For the following match, Catcheside provided the accountant with the following expense sheet:

price of 2nd class ticket Newcastle/Euston	£2.19s.11d
use of toilet facilities at Euston	1d
TOTAL	£3.00s.00d

It seems that the situation came to a head at the end of the Fifties when one respected international decided to return to his home town to be treated by a local physiotherapist. In those days it was deemed necessary to take only one or two extra players in tow in case of mishaps (not a back-up team of regimental proportions as is the case today). The player concerned felt that he should be reimbursed for the treatment received whilst the administrators were adamant that the Union's physiotherapist in Cardiff should have been utilised. A stand-off ensued. The player held his ground and, approximately an hour prior to kick-off in an away international, insisted that he would take the field only if he were paid what he felt was his due. In the end, this was forthcoming, the player took his place in the starting line-up and Wales won the game.

Thank goodness that this attitude has been consigned to the history books and rugby players are accorded the respect and salaries which they deserve. The Scarlets can be justly proud that they have embraced this professional ethic.

11

Lewis Jones

Miracle worker

The date was March 9, 1957 and I was sitting on the back seat of my father's Sunbeam Talbot on my way to my very first rugby international match at Cardiff. A more accurate description of my condition would be that I was wedged in between Ronald Francis (Chairman of Brynaman RFC) and his son Edward. My discomfort, however, was nothing compared with my excitement at the prospect that lay ahead.

My father, grandfather (who was allocated the passenger seat next to my dad) and Mr Francis were involved in an animated conversation comparing the skills of the (then) current players with former heroes. The names of people like Bleddyn Williams, Haydn Tanner, Cliff Jones, Jackie Kyle and Jeff Butterfield were mentioned regularly. However, one player's name, Lewis Jones, kept coming up time and time again. My grandfather maintained, and Mr Francis (chairman of the local club and therefore a knowledgeable person) agreed, that Lewis Jones truly was a genius and at times his playing was 'miraculous'. Apparently he was able to whip the crowd into a frenzy just by running out onto the pitch. Now if my grandfather said all these things about this player he must indeed have been 'something special'.

As a nine-year-old, my experience of the word 'miraculous' was confined to a Sunday when it was used by our minister, the Reverend Gerallt Jones at Gibea Chapel, Brynaman. To my young mind, the term was synonymous with events described in the Bible – events such as the Feeding of the Five Thousand and the Healing of Jairus's Daughter. I had never before heard the adjective used to describe the skills of a rugby player!

In later years, I was to hear an amusing story of a certain gentleman who had what is now described as an 'industrial accident'. He in fact slipped and fell over while at work, hit his head on some concrete, spent time in the local hospital and on discharge decided to sue his employers for negligence.

He duly won the case and was awarded a substantial amount of damages. One of the insurance assessors, however, was not convinced that this had been a bona fide claim and challenged the claimant as they were leaving the court house. 'I know you're pulling a fast one,' he said to the jubilant man, 'and I'm going to follow you for the rest of your days just to prove my point.' 'You're welcome,' came the reply, 'I'll tell you what I'm going to do during the next week or so. From here I'm going to catch the five o'clock to Paddington (first class of course) and I'll be spending the night at the Ritz in Piccadilly. Tomorrow morning I'm booked (also first class) with Air France to Charles de

Gaulle in Paris and after lunch at the George V, I have a reservation on the TGV to Lourdes for the miracle!'

To return to the miracle associated with Lewis Jones. Benjamin Lewis Jones won his first international cap when he played for the Welsh schoolboys (under the captaincy of Carwyn James) against France at Cardiff. The news that he had won his first cap was broken to the youngster by his headmaster at Gowerton Grammar School during the school assembly. The young man had reputedly just put down his viola when he was called forward. The announcement was made to a very proud and excited school hall.

Lewis Jones handing off Noel Henderson in Dublin, 1952, when Wales won the Triple Crown.

After leaving school in July 1948, Lewis Jones then started on his period of National Service and joined the Royal Navy. He played for Devenport Services and represented the Navy against the Army at Twickenham. His performances at these matches attracted the attention of the 'Big Five', and so it was that in January 1950, when he was just 18 years and 9 months of age, Lewis was chosen to play at fullback for Wales. It is interesting to note that Lewis was two months younger than Haydn Tanner, another product of Gowerton Grammar School, when he won his first cap.

To say that Wales's record against England at Twickenham during this period was disastrous is something of an understatement. Wales had won only once at Twickers in forty years – that victory was in 1933 when they won by 7-3 thanks to a try and a drop goal by Ronnie Boon. It was no surprise therefore that England were again clear favourites to win. Tickets for the match were at a premium even though the price had been increased from 10 to 15 shillings in order to finance the building of a new East Stand. Such was the demand that Lewis was unable to secure a ticket for his own father. Help was at hand in the shape of Mr Eric Evans, Secretary of the WRU, who offered to sacrifice his seat in the stand for standing room on the terraces!

It was a very nervous Lewis Jones who ran out in front of 75,000 vociferous supporters on that January day at Twickenham. While the teams lined up for the anthems, the Welsh captain John Gwilliam whispered a few words of encouragement in the youngster's ear and by kick-off the butterflies in Lewis's stomach had completely flown away.

England were the first to score when, after eight minutes, the wing John Smith intercepted a pass and ran some forty yards to score the first try. Just before half-time, a kick from the England fullback Hofmeyr dropped short of the halfway line. Now, if he had read the coaching manual of the day, Lewis would have kicked the ball safely into touch.

To the astonishment of his captain, twenty-nine fellow players, one referee, two touch judges and 75,000 spectators, the young fullback set off and created one of the most amazing tries ever witnessed on the hallowed turf of HQ. It was a try worthy of that scored by Prince Obolensky against New Zealand in 1936.

After gathering the ball, Lewis Jones realised that the England defence were somewhat pedestrian and were slow to the tackle area. This gave him enough time to cross the advantage line where he found himself with acres of space to manoeuvre. By this time the whole of Twickenham was on its feet in anticipation and the noise was deafening. Unabashed, Jones then managed to hypnotise the opposition with two dummies before he was finally tackled. But this was after he had managed to hand on to Malcolm Thomas who found Bob Evans in support. The Newport back-row forward made ground before distributing to Cliff Davies (Kenfig Hill and Cardiff) who claimed the try. It was a score that went down in the annals of rugby history – a try that secured a win for Wales by 11-5 and a try that eventually led to a Grand Slam. Little wonder, therefore, that the captain, John Gwilliam, and the boy wonder, Lewis Jones, were carried shoulder high off the field by their ecstatic supporters.

It was also no surprise that Lewis was a strong candidate for the Lions party to tour Australia and New Zealand in the summer of 1950. He was not selected initially, but was called up to join the squad following an injury to George Norton. He took full advantage of the opportunity and produced an outstanding performance at Eden Park, Auckland on July 29, 1950. The All Blacks were victorious by 11-8 to the delight of the 60,000 local supporters who had witnessed an epic encounter. The New Zealand captain Peter Johnstone said in his aftermatch speech that this had been the best game he had ever had the privilege of taking part in. The Lions were led by Bleddyn Williams and the philosophy preached to the team before each match was 'attack is the best form of defence'. This was music to the ears of the young viola player and the try he created for the Olympic sprinter Ken Jones (Newport) is amongst the finest of the century as recorded by the New Zealand Weekly News.

The Lions decided to run the ball from their own goal-line as they had realised that the All Blacks were positioned for the kick into touch. An ensuing scrum saw the outside half, Jackie Kyle, throw a rushed pass to Bleddyn Williams. The ball did not reach the centre three-quarter as Lewis Jones had suddenly appeared from nowhere and was now dancing his way through the opposition and racing towards the halfway line. The young fullback could not believe his eyes – the field had opened up in front of him and was now as wide and spacious as the Serengeti! A quick glance to the right confirmed that the ever-reliable Ken Jones was at his shoulder. Then came the *coup de grâce*. A few yards further on Lewis came head to head with Bob Scott, the finest fullback of his generation. Undeterred he presented Ken Jones with a perfect pass and from the New Zealand ten-yard line, it proved an easy run-in for the Olympian, with Henderson and Roper, the All Black three-quarters, being mere spectators. Without doubt this was one of international rugby's finest moments.

Lewis's skills are well documented in the excellent book which commemorates the history of Welsh rugby, *Fields of Praise*. To quote Professors David Smith and Gareth Williams:

> Jones possessed phenomenal kicking skills (at which he worked assiduously), scorching speed, a mesmerizing variation of pace and stride, hips that oscillated as if on ball-bearings, and shoulders that shrugged and twisted through thickets of tacklers.

Lewis Jones played for Llanelli for two seasons before changing codes and joined Leeds where he would stay for twelve years. During this time he broke all club records when he scored 505 points in season 1956/57. At Stradey he was as much a hero as Albert Jenkins had been in the Twenties. It was this innate ability to create the unexpected, to mesmerize as well as entertain the crowds that embodied the talent that was B.L. Jones – truly a miracle worker.

Another try for Lewis and Leeds at Wembley.

12

Ray Williams

The original version

Ray Wiliams played in the scarlet jersey of Llanelli for sixteen seasons. He completed 450 games and scored 213 tries. By any standards this is an honourable record and one of which he can be justly proud.

I recently spent a very enjoyable afternoon in the company of this affable gentleman at his home in Hedley Terace, Llanelli. Indeed, such was his enthusiasm, verve and apparent physical fitness that he might well be able to withstand the might of the All Blacks even today. I'm sure that if the International Olympic Committee were to organise a 100-metre dash for the over 75s, Ray Williams would be on the winner's podium.

His first match at Stradey Park was against Penarth on Good Friday 1946, whilst his last match was prematurely brought to an end through injury at Ynysangharad Park in April 1961. During the Annual General Meeting held at Stradey a month later, it was decided that Ray would be made a Life Member of the club, the first player to receive such an honour. This was in appreciation of his commitment, honesty and outstanding performances.

During Ray's sojourn at Stradey Park, the team experienced many highs and lows on the field. Off the field, however, team spirit was indomitable. Whatever the financial and administrative difficulties behind the scenes, there was an optimistic attitude amongst the squad. They felt that things could only get better. Ray Williams was a primary force in this period and led by example. Success would be achieved through hard work and perseverance; coupled with occasional flashes of genius and exciting playmaking, how could they fail? This strategy is one that has been implemented at the club over the last fifty years.

Ray Williams would agree that he is a home bird and he considered Stradey Park his second home. A move to another club was not an option, even if this meant forfeiting a collection of Welsh caps. It may be that the three caps gained while playing at Llanelli would have been thirty or more had he chosen to play at Cardiff or Newport. Be that as it may, Ray was happy to don the shirts of Llanelli and Wales, but I suspect it was the former that was closer to his heart.

During his period as Physical Edcation teacher at Gwendraeth Grammar School, Ray had a major influence on the development of some of the best rugby players of the twentieth century. The academy at Drefach produced such players as Robert Morgan, D. Ken Jones, Barry John and Gareth Davies; the four starting their careers at Stradey and then moving on to represent their country. Ken, Barry and Gareth in due course became British Lions. All four recognise the huge debt of gratitude they owe Ray Williams, who was their mentor in their formative years.

There is an amusing story involving Ray and D. Ken Jones. The occasion was a match played between Llanelli and Nuneaton on Easter Saturday 1960 (Scarlets 42 Nuneaton 0). During this period Ken was a sixth-form pupil at Gwendraeth Grammar School with Ray being his sports master. As the match proceeded Ken was heard to shout during a typical Ray Williams burst upfield, 'Sir, Sir . . . pass it out now!'

Ray Williams won his first cap against Scotland at St Helen's in Swansea in 1954. It was the last match of the Five Nations Championship to be played at this historic ground. Wales won 15-3 with Ray being one of the try scorers. During this period Wales boasted a glut of talented wingers – players of the calibre of Ken Jones, Trevor Brewer, Malcolm Thomas, Gareth Griffiths, Gwyn Rowlands, and Haydn Morris. Once again, however, the selectors stand accused of ignoring players from the west; a case proven by the measly number of caps awarded to Ray Williams. It would be another three years before he again represented his country. This time France was the opposition and the game, which was held at Stade Colombes, saw Wales 19-13 victors with Llanelli supplying both wing three-quarters – Ray on the right wing and

Ray Williams – the first to the loose ball against New Zealand, November 1953.

the elusive Geoff Howells on the left. His third and final game for his country was against Australia in January 1958. The occasion was noteworthy on two counts – Wales won the match by 9 points to 3 and of the fifteen players represented, six of them came from Llanelli. At fullback was Terry Davies, Cyril Davies at centre, Ray Williams on the left wing, Carwyn James and Wynne Evans were the half-backs while R.H. Williams took his customary place in the second row. It was a day to savour.

Slippery, cunning, fleet-footed – some of the adjectives used to describe Ray Williams's style of play. Whether he played in the centre or on the wing, he was adept at penetrating weaknesses in the opposition. He had an uncanny knack of seeing potential gaps on the field and was able to capitalise on any hesitancy in the opposing defence with lightning speed. Speed is an asset for a wing three-quarter at any level, as seen on any given Saturday at Tregaron, Tondu or Tonyrefail. However to play at the highest level, a player needs to be able to add a little extra with the right choice of running angles, quick acceleration off the mark and an overview of what is happening around him. This is where Ray came into his own.

According to his peers, Ray had something of the chess grandmaster about him. He was something of a Spasky or Fischer. Whereas those of us who play chess purely for recreational purposes only anticipate the next move, the professionals spend a great deal of time debating and pondering. The experts see a move merely as a small part of the bigger picture, as a means of attaining the final goal. That is the way Ray played his rugby.

During our teatime conversation I asked him what he thought of the players of his generation. Who had created the biggest impression? To my surprise they were three Englishmen: Jeff Butterfield and Lewis Cannell, the Northampton centres and the Coventry wing Peter Jackson – a genius in Ray's eyes. There was also one local player who always impressed him. One Hubert Daniels from Pontyberem who played briefly for Llanelli. 'If he was playing today, every European club would be after him. I never saw anyone so capable of bringing out the best in other players.'

This last comment encapsulates perfectly Ray's own achievements. It is typical of the modesty of the man that he disregards his own immeasurable contribution to the giants of the game in Wales. Ray Williams is still an ever-present figure at Stradey Park and a stalwart of Llanelli Male Voice Choir – but that's another story!

13

R.H.

The giant from Cwmllynfell

My father must have decided one day that nine was a good age to introduce one's son to the wonders of international sport. I base this conclusion on the fact that I was nine years old when I attended my first rugby international at the Arms Park (Wales vs Ireland) and that in the summer of 1957 I found myself again on a highway, this time the A40 rather than the A48, on my way to St John's Wood in London. The venue was Lord's Cricket Ground and the opposing teams were England and the West Indies. I was on my way to watch my first Test Match.

Not for us the exclusive enclosure in front of the pavilion nor were we lucky enough to get seats in the stands. No, we were part of an orderly queue, hoping and praying that we would be fortunate enough to get into the ground.

Our patience was finally rewarded, and just as the umpires strode out onto the hallowed turf, my father and I settled down on the grass just to the left of the pavilion and waited for the first ball of the day to be bowled. The team sheets for the match read like a *Who's Who* of test cricket and featured the likes of Kanhai, Sobers, Ramadhin, Valentine, Worrell, Weekes, Walcott, and O.G. Smith for the West Indies; Graveney, May, Cowdrey, Bailey, Trueman and Statham for England. To see these players in the flesh, and at such close quarters, was a dream come true for a Welsh lad of tender years.

The day as a whole proved to be an unforgettable one with many high points. However, the climax was reached towards the close of play. England had batted first and, thanks to a partnership of 180 between Colin Cowdrey and Godfrey Evans, had amassed a sizeable total for their first innings. Peter May and his team were therefore quietly confident they would be in a commanding position. But they had reckoned without the genius of Everton Weekes. The West Indies were in dire straits and it needed a masterly display from one of the Caribbean superstars to salvage the situation. Thus it was that at ten minutes to six on that Friday evening Everton de Courtenay Weekes found himself leaving the sanctuary of the Long Room to face the onslaught of the England bowlers. As he made his way to the cricket square, I followed his progress through a pair of Ross binoculars. Weekes must have been all of 5ft 6in tall, but there was something in his demeanour and his gait which conveyed a sense of discipline, self-assurance and all-round magnetism that belied his shortness of stature.

Within minutes of his arrival at the crease, the largely partisan English crowd had been stirred into action. A ripple of excitement was palpable around the ground. Almost immediately the English bowling attack was treated with disdain: a square cut here caused the ball to torpedo its way to the boundary; a short delivery there from Fred Trueman was treated with equal ferocity. And so it went on with runs flowing in a torrent. The came the *coup de grâce*. Trevor Bailey's delivery was accurate in both line and length but Weekes danced his way down the wicket, hit the ball sweetly in the middle of the bat and the ensuing four runs left the England fielders dumbstruck. When Emrys Davies called time on the day's play, Weekes had scored 42 majestic runs. He went on to reach a total of 90 with a masterful display of attacking strokeplay coupled with no small degree of elegance.

What, you might ask is the connection between Everton Weekes's performance at Lord's and Stradey Park? Charisma, determination, authority, presence are all qualities attributed to the Caribbean genius. But they are equally pertinent when used to describe one of the Llanelli greats who played

The line-out master.

for the Scarlets, Wales and the British Lions during the 1950s. I refer of course to R.H. Williams. Without doubt Rhys is the best second-row forward ever to have played for either Wales or the British Lions. I appreciate that not everyone would agree with this statement. Some would favour Willie John McBride, Martin Johnson or Gordon Brown but the general consensus amongst commentators, players and supporters favours the Cwmllynfell superman. The expression 'simply the best' could have been penned exclusively for R.H.

After a dazzling display during the 1959 Lions tour of New Zealand, Tiny Hill and Colin Meads were heard to declare that if R.H. had been born in the land of the white cloud, there was no question that he would have worn the All Black shirt. High praise indeed from such giants of the game. The same sentiments were echoed in South Africa by such venerated players as van

Wyk, Claassens and du Rand. It is also true to say that R.H. Williams's name would have been included in any dream team chosen from past and present players. The young man brought up in the village of Cwmllynfell on the edge of the Black Mountain had indeed come a long way.

The determination to succeed manifested itself early on, both on and off the rugby field. After leaving Ystalyfera Grammar School, the young R.H. Williams then went on to study at Aberystwyth University. Although the academic world beckoned, it was his love of sport that came to the fore. His first cap was gained playing against Ireland at Dublin in 1954. Wales won by a single point thanks to a last minute drop goal from Llanelli centre, Denzil Thomas, the original one-cap wonder who having won the match for his country lost his place in the team!

What were the qualities which made R.H. Williams such an outstanding forward? Physical and mental strength, technique, stamina, bravery, resilience, a fighting never-say-die spirit, endurance, the ability to influence others, commitment – all of these could be applied to R.H. These attributes were on display whether he played at Eden Park, Twickenham, Ellis Park, Stradey or at Cwmllynfell. He was an ideal role model for the younger generation of rugby players.

To some followers of the game it is the darting runs and skilful sidesteps of the backs which engender the most excitement in a game. However, for the true purist, it is the hard graft of the forwards which deserve the plaudits. The last word goes to Carwyn James and John Reason who wrote in the *The World of Rugby*:

> Rhys Williams was that rarity among British locks, a world class player. Of all the positions in a rugby team, lock forward has been that in which British rugby has found it most difficult to match the forwards produced by South Africa, New Zealand and, in latter years, France. But as Colin Meads himself says, Rhys Williams was a champion. Meads rates Rhys Williams and Johan Claassen as the best two locks he played against with Benoit Dauga not far behind.

Praise indeed!

14

Terry Davies

A genius

As I flick through the faded programmes of the good old days I see you: powerfully built, five foot eleven and thirteen-and-a-half stone. Fair haired and smiling, I salute you Terrence John, the shy and unassuming Barbarian of 1957, and Lion of 1959, always a gentleman, on and off the field. A fiercely proud Welshman who was, somehow, listed T. E. in all the programmes. My Arthur, my Glyndŵr, my hero at Stradey Park.

On Saturday afternoons I stand awestruck amidst the razor-sharp wits on the Tanner Bank: the knowledgeable crowd celebrate a titan who triumphed over injury and loss. The brilliant entertainer, fearless on the field, a giant running with giants: Carwyn, R. H. Onllwyn and Ray . . . and Llew.

The quintessential fullback of your generation, you swoop like an eagle to scoop up every stray ball. Fourteen scarlet-blooded men and you, charged with defending the line from the infidel. Our last line of defence and you never shirked a tackle; our first line of attack and you never missed an opportunity. Broad shoulders, safe hands, sound boots, infallible from forty yards.

Twickenham 1958 and I missed it.

'Too young', said dad.

'Too far', said mam.

'Too expensive', thought I.

It was a drawn game, three points all. And one last chance. A fifty yarder against the wind for victory and the Triple Crown, but the crossbar denied us that victory. That crossbar was severed and brought back to Wales and to West Wales, scarred and bearing your signature.

You were a sawyer by trade and accomplished in the workshop. That workshop offered a replacement crossbar but the offer was spurned. The legend of the Twickenham crossbar will survive as folk memory and the memory of the champion of champions will be cherished by the timid, tongue-tied teenager on the Tanner Bank.

The words of Professor David Thorne, formerly of Llangennech, and a great admirer of the talent of Terry Davies from Bynea, one of the all-time great rugby fullbacks. He represented the Lions in New Zealand in 1959, starring in the second test (lost 8-11) and in the fourth test (victorious 9-6). According to journalists covering the tour, including Terry McLean of New Zealand, Terry Davies was the compete master of his craft. At the end of that tour, the All-Blacks players in a special tribute to Terry stated that he would secure his place in any international rugby team in the world.

Terry crossing the line against Neath at the Gnoll.

15

D.K. and D.B.D.

Two free spirits

There have been many famous 'duos': Morecambe and Wise, Tate and Lyle, Marks and Spencer to name but a few. To this list I would like to add my own combination namely Davies and Jones. 'Who on earth are they?' I hear you ask. I refer to Brian Davies and Ken Jones who represented Llanelli with some distinction in midfield during the 1960s.

I was a pupil at Amman Valley Grammar School in Ammanford when I first saw these two play together. Our Religious Instruction teacher, Mr Bryn Roberts, had organised a school trip to the Arms Park at Cardiff where the Welsh Secondary Schools were to take on their French counterparts. Now considering that not one boy from our school was included in the national side, this seems a bizarre decision. However, Mr Roberts was one of the team selectors and felt that the least he could do was ensure a reasonable crowd was in attendance. As a result, on April 30,1960 we were on our way to Cardiff to see the match.

What I witnessed on the field of play is still etched on my memory. The whole crowd was mesmerised by the display put on by Brian, a Llanelli

WELSH SEC. SCHOOLS		FRENCH SCHOLAIRES
Colours: RED		*Colours:* BLUE
1 R. G. BAYLIS *(Tonyrefail G.S.)*	Full Back	15 G. MARCHADOU *(Stade Aurillacois)*
2 H. L. JONES *(Barry County)*	Right Wing Left	14 G. SEGUIN *(Stade Cadurcien)*
3 D. B. DAVIES *(Llanelly G.S.)*	Right Centre Left	13 M. SABATHIE *(St. Vincent)*
4 E. JAMES *(Pontardawe G.S.)*	Left Centre Right	12 J. CADAUGADE *(Peyrehorade)*
5 M. MORGAN *(Brynmawr G.S.)*	Left Wing Right	11 L. COUDEYRE *(Montferrandaise)*
6 D. K. JONES *(Captain)* *(Gwendraeth G.S.)*	Outside Half	10 P. CLAUERIE *(Toulouse)*
7 B. J. WILLIAMS *(Bridgend County)*	Inside Half	9 R. ANTONUCCIO *(Beziers)*
8 J. YOUNG *(Garw G.S.)*	Forwards	2 J. BIDEGARAY *(La Perolliere)*
9 C. R. WILLIAMS *(Tonypandy G.S.)*		1 Y. YACONO *(Ussel)*
10 C. JONES *(Pontypridd G.S.)*		3 G. RASCOL *(Mazametain)*
11 D. K. EDWARDS *(Bridgend County)*		4 P. CHAINIER *(Angoulene)*
12 C. S. DUTSON *(Grove Park)*		5 J. CONTI *(Stade Toulousain)*
13 K. G. BROWN *(Haverfordwest G.S.)*		7 G. DUHOMEZ *(Bressane)*
14 D. HUGHES *(Pengam G.S.)*	Referee:	6 L. PORCHIER *(U.S. Romanaise)*
15 F. OWEN *(Quakers Yard G.S.)*	Mr. F. G. PRICE, W.R.U. (Blaenavon)	8 S. DUNET *(U.S. Bergeracoise)*

D. Ken Jones crossing for a memorable individual try for the Lions against South Africa in 1962.

Grammar schoolboy and Ken Jones, who hailed from Gwendraeth Grammar School. I had been raised on a diet of Bleddyn Williams (Cardiff) and Peter Jackson (Coventry). According to my father and grandfather, these were the gold standard by which any other backs had to be judged. Their skills were unsurpassed: in speed, swerve or sidestep, no one, apparently, could match these two players.

But Ken Jones and Brian Davies were true athletes who could cover 100 yards in under 10 seconds. Coupled with this speed were all the attributes deemed necesssary in players who can perform at the highest level. I was well and truly convinced that here was the kind of genius I had heard about at home.

A week later, the two were in action again. This time for Llanelli in the Snelling Sevens Tournament again at the Arms Park in front of 30,000 fans. In a fairy-tale ending, Llanelli won the trophy for the first time in their history with the two schoolboys playing a major part in the victory. When Onllwyn Brace, the Scarlets captain, raised the cup aloft, the whole stadium erupted, supporters and journalists alike impressed with the spectacle they had witnessed.

The following seasons saw a huge increase in the number of spectators travelling to Stradey Park to watch the exploits of the new young members of the team – a scenario repeated wherever new charismatic and talented players develop. One only has to think of Ryan Giggs or David Beckham at Manchester United, Billy Boston at Wigan or Matthew Maynard at Glamorgan cricket.

When my family and I moved to live in Neath during the 1980s, I became friendly with Mr Haydn Morris, a deacon at Soar Maes-yr-Haf, our local chapel. Mr Morris was as fanatical and knowledgeable about cricket as it is possible for any person to be. While I sang the praises of Ian Botham, he was a little more reticent: compared with Wally Hammond or Keith Miller, Botham wasn't even in contention! That is until Mr and Mrs Morris went on holiday to Taunton a few weeks later – where a cricket match at the County Ground proved too much of a temptation for Mr Morris . . . When we next met up, he rushed forward excitedly and described the most memorable innings he had ever seen, courtesy of one Ian Botham. The Morrises could not wait to return to Taunton to watch more of the same!

It was this same feeling that Ken Jones and Brian Davies stirred amongst Scarlets' supporters who flocked to Stradey for a period of three years. There was certainly a telepathic understanding between the two players as exemplified in a match between Llanelli and Aberavon in the early Sixties. Brian gathered the ball more or less on his own try-line and after beating his opposing centre on the outside, he then swerved inside and made for the 25-yard line where the Wizards fullback was about to make a cover tackle. At the very last instant Brian transferred to Ken who hared for the Aberavon try-line like an express train. He covered the 80-odd yards in seconds with the Stradey faithful lost for words.

A series of serious injuries brought Brian's career to a premature end. He gained three caps for his country, one of which was against Scotland where he was on the field of play for 80 minutes without receiving a single pass. The Wales captain Clive Rowlands decided that the only way his team would win was if play was confined to the forwards. The ploy worked; Wales won the match but Brian was inexplicably dropped from the team and replaced by Meirion Roberts. I'm convinced that if Brian had decided to play on the wing for Wales during that period, then his international career would have been a long and illustrious one.

D.K. Jones will forever be remembered for scoring one of the finest individual tries ever scored for the British Lions in a test match. At Ellis Park, Johannesburg in 1962, the Cross Hands centre three-quarter received a pass near the Lions 25-yard line. He took off at a rate of knots, sidestepping off his right foot and leaving the South African tacklers in his wake. With the Springbok fullback approaching, Jones changed gear, accelerated like a jaguar for the line, and with a dive reminiscent of Greg Luganis, plunged over for the try.

Yes, there have been many well-known duos *à la* Lindwall and Miller, but it has to be said that Davies and Jones were also something rather special.

Brian Davies in his playing days.

16

What of Terry Price?

Oozing talent . . .

To describe the discussion as a heated one would be to exaggerate; lively or animated would be a better choice of adjective for the evening's debate. The venue was a hotel bar in the Recoleta district of Buenos Aires and the exchange took place during Wales's tour to Argentina in June 2004. As a nation, the Welsh consider themselves an authority when it comes to defining what makes a great rugby player, a great team or a great coach. To this end, and as in all rugby debates, we make sure that our voice is heard loud and clear on this subject.

You can imagine the scene, therefore, on that night in Buenos Aires when ten of us media 'experts' came together to compile a list of the maestros and geniuses of the game. Gareth, Gerald, Barry, Phil, Bleddyn, Jonathan, Albert, Cliff (Jones and Morgan), Bancroft, Gould, the James brothers and Lewis Jones were all obvious choices. Strange as it may seem neither Robert nor Gwyn Jones were familiar with the exploits of the talented Arthur 'Monkey' Gould. Then again, as his career was at its peak during the reign of Queen Victoria, they could be excused their ignorance!

Gareth Charles was particularly upset to find that not one of his beloved Pontypridd team had been included but was soon cheered when he realised that two pupils from his former *alma mater* had been included. Indeed his mood had lifted to such an extent that he bought the next round of drinks! Huw Llewellyn Davies was of course more than happy with many of the names and in particular with that of his neighbour from Upper Coelbren Road in Gwaun-cae-gurwen, Gareth Edwards.

It was at this point that Clive Rowlands, who had up until now been engrossed in the produce of the vineyards of Mendoza, threw his hat into the ring. 'Listen boys, I've been sitting here for over an hour listening to what you've got to say, and I'm amazed that not one of you has mentioned Terry Price. He should be in the top ten of the best ever Welsh rugby players. If you're talking about raw talent, a strength to rival 'superman', and an ability through sleight of hand and quickness of thought to bamboozle the opposition then Terry's your man. He had it all.' Silence descended over the group as we contemplated Clive's words. As a former player, coach and manager himself, he should know and who were we to argue!

I was a lad of fourteen when I first saw Terry Price play rugby. The venue was the Llanelli Grammar School playing fields and we the Amman Valley Grammar School, were the visitors. Several of us had travelled to Llanelli to support our school against what was arguably the finest schoolboy rugby team in Great Britain at that time. Even then, Terry Price stood out amongst his peers. Physically, he was a man amongst boys and his talent was quite remarkable. I witnessed this at close quarters from the touchline. Unfortunately for me, the appointed touch judge was unable to carry out his duties and I was roped in to substitute.

We were only twenty minutes into the first half when I started cursing this man-mountain in the Llanelli back line. Every time the referee awarded a penalty to Llanelli and after each and every try, the same scenario would repeat itself. I would be standing behind the goal posts in a zombie-like trance watching incredulously as the ball went sailing between the uprights. Then, to add insult to injury, the prevailing wind would carry the ball even further in the direction of the town centre. Now this would not have been a problem if the two touch judges had been of a similar disposition but in this case the other gentleman must have been at least sixty years of age, and so it fell to me to retrieve the said ball every time! It's a day that I will not forget in a hurry – my first sighting of a superstar on a rugby field.

It was a year later that I again witnessed an exceptional performance from Terry. He was a still a pupil at Llanelli Grammar School, but now he had graduated to playing for Llanelli at Stradey Park. The opposition on that last day of December 1963 was no one less than Wilson Whineray's All Blacks. Picture the scene a few days prior to the game: Terry Price the sixth-former standing in the headmaster's study and asking Mr Stan Rees for permission to play against New Zealand!

To return to the match. Llanelli found themselves leading the All Blacks 8-3 at half-time. This was due in no small part to the superhuman effort of the forwards, led by their inspirational captain, Marlston Morgan. The sports writer of the *Llanelly Star* noted:

> After dominating the first half it looked as if they might well pull it off. The Llanelly forwards showed the way with a rip-roaring display. They kept up on the ball like tigers and were on top of a New Zealander as soon as he gained possession.

Unfortunately things did not quite go Llanelli's way in the second half. Whether as a result of Whineray's half-time team talk or the fact that fate played a hand, the visitors managed to gain the upper hand. An injury to wing Robert Morgan and outside half Beverley Davies with only five minutes played of the second half left the Scarlets in a state of disarray. Not only was victory against the best team in the world an uphill struggle, it was in the best cinematic traditions of Tom Cruise's 'Mission Impossible'. The final result was a resounding victory to the All Blacks by 22-8. A cursory glance at the New Zealand teamsheet for the match tells us all we need to know about the visitors' quality: Mac Herewini, Malcolm Dick, Ian McRae, Pat Walsh, Ralph Caulton, Bruce Watt, Chris Laidlaw, Wilson Whineray (captain), Dennis Young, Ken Gray, Colin Meads, Kevin Barry, Dave Graham, Brian Lochore, Waka Nathan.

Little wonder therefore that the Scarlets weren't victorious even though they had given a good account of themselves in the opening period. As the crowds filed from the ground after the final whistle, the talk amongst the ranks of the Llanelli faithful and journalists alike was all of one player – the sixth-former from Llanelli Grammar School. Immediately comparisons were made with Haydn Tanner and Willie Davies, both schoolboys when they faced Jack Manchester's All Blacks for Swansea in 1935.

Terry Price came from a line of talented sportsmen, his grandfather Dai Hiddlestone having been a cornerstone of the Neath team, while his brothers, Gareth, Geraint and Iwan, were also gifted players. From the moment the young Terry ran onto the rugby field, one could sense his charisma and overall presence. Where others would be fired up with the expectation of the confrontation, it seemed that the only thing that flowed through his veins was confidence. The bigger the occasion and the larger the crowd, the better was his performance. This was exemplified in that match against New Zealand. When Beverley Davies was stretchered off the field, Terry was moved from the wing to play at outside half. Towards the end of the match, the wing forward Waka Nathan made a dash for the try-line to score what appeared to be a certain try.

Preparing for a training session
with the British Universities.

He had reckoned without the crunching tackle which ensued – a tackle which, although perfectly legitimate, left the All Black with a broken jaw. The victory may have gone to New Zealand but the plaudits from Hendy to Hamilton were for the Scarlets and especially Terry Price.

In latter years we became close friends as we travelled regularly to report on various Rugby League matches. I was always struck by the warmth of the welcome we received on these visits and the high esteem in which Terry was obviously held. On one such occasion we were staying at a London Hotel prior to a Rugby League Challenge Cup Final match at Wembley. The effect of too much alcohol was taking its toll on several of the fans present and they were vociferous in their condemnation of many leading Welsh players who they felt had not performed well during the international season. Terry declined to take part in the discussion and retired to his bed. I had got to know him well enough by this time to realise that it was not in his nature to condemn fellow players – his philosophy was to highlight an individual's strengths rather can concentrate unduly on weaknesses.

He went on to win eight Welsh caps from 1965-67 and was part of the successful squad who won the Triple Crown during season 1964/65. A contract with Bradford Northern saw him play league rugby from 1967 onwards until, in the twilight of his career, he ventured into the realms of American Football, playing for the Buffalo Bills.

As far as his own career was concerned, he confessed that his only regret was that he had played too much sport at an early age and not given his body enough time to develop and mature. Terry Price passed away in April 1993 as a result of a road-traffic accident in Oxford. Clive Rowlands was absolutely correct in his declaration on that night in Buenos Aires and I, together with thousands of Llanelli supporters, have to agree – Terry Price was one of the best.

Another successful kick in the colours of Bradford Northern.

52

17

Barry John

Still the King

Nijinsky, Michelangelo, Muhammad Ali, Galileo Galilei, Edmund Hillary, William Shakespeare, Johan Cruyff, The Great Wall of China, Enrico Caruso, Aristotle, Joan of Arc, Phidippides, Christopher Columbus, Nelson Mandela, William Blake, Pablo Picasso, Frank Lloyd Wright, the Beatles, Leonardo da Vinci, Mount Everest, James Joyce, Wolfgang Amadeus Mozart, Barry John.

What an auspicious list! It was the winning entry in a competition held by *The Observer* during the late 1990s where the task was to write not more than a hundred words on a sporting hero. The winner was one James Davy of Auckland, New Zealand.

The vast majority of rugby supporters worldwide associate Barry John with Cardiff Rugby Football Club. This is where the foundations were laid for his legendary partnership with Gareth Edwards and where he spent most of his rugby-playing career. However, it was in the scarlet jersey of Llanelli that Barry first played premier club rugby. Like many a famous player before him, he donned the Llanelli strip while still a pupil at Gwendraeth Grammar School, subsequently representing the club for three seasons during the Sixties.

His slight physical frame belied the talent that was to blossom at Stradey Park during that time. It was impossible to categorise Barry; it was impossible to predict his next move. According to Carwyn James and John Reason in their excellent publication *The World of Rugby*, 'he was completely unaware of the organisational technique of rugby football. He just was not interested. He created a personal privacy which was so complete that no coach ever thought of intruding.'

He possessed the consummate artistry and single-mindedness associated with the true greats. Added to this was a gritty determination born of his upbringing in the coal-mining community of Cefneithin. It is easy to see that here was a genius, a master of his craft, as perfectly at ease on his local village ground as in any of the world's famous arenas. He played a large part in the Llanelli victory against Australia at Stradey in 1966 but he himself considers the try against France at Stade Colombes in 1971 as one of his finest. It was a Grand Slam decider for both teams.

It was a full-blooded encounter. It would need a superhuman individual effort to settle the contest. Up stepped Jeff Young, the Welsh hooker, who unexpectedly took a strike against the head with the scrum positioned in front of the French posts. The ball was jettisoned back to the outside half who, in an instant, spotted a gap between Berot and Bertranne in the French midfield defence. They seriously

King John.

underestimated Barry's speed over the first ten yards and quick as a flash he was over the try-line. This was a pivotal moment in the match which Wales went on to win and with it the Grand Slam for the first time since season 1951/52.

No one has ever had a keener awareness of the opposition's jugular than Barry John. He had an uncanny knack of sizing up and exploiting weakness. This was admirably demonstrated during the British Lions tour of New Zealand in 1971. The All Blacks were much the stronger team in the first test match but were unable to make inroads into the Lions' territory thanks to a masterly display of tactical kicking from the Lions No. 10. John Reason and Carwyn James take up the story:

> He pulled McCormick, the New Zealand fullback, from one side of the field to the other with a string of merciless kicks that almost cut the lines. McCormick in fact did incredibly well to get as close to them as he did. It was a miracle of positioning and running for him to be able to get near enough to the kicks to stoop and reach for them, but they were almost always just out of his reach, and as he slithered and fumbled, he looked like a player who had come to the end of the international road.

The British and Irish Lions went on to win the match and the series – a record still unsurpassed in the modern game. The Lions and all of New Zealand thereafter called him 'The King'.

Barry's individual try on that 1971 tour against New Zealand Universities was simply unbelievable. He received the ball from a scrummage just outside the oppostion 22 and in front of the posts. He stood still for a split second and then feinted to drop for goal. The opposition approached, moving in as if to charge down the effort. However, Barry glided past the defenders, moving towards his two centres Dawes and Gibson. He showed the ball to the next defender, came off his left foot leaving others groping thin air. Frank Keating describes in his book *The Great Number Tens* how the crowd was stunned into silence as B.J. 'tiptoed delicately' underneath the posts. Keating also quotes Carwyn James in the chapter; a quotation particularly relevant in relation to the try just described:

> Instinct, intuition, call it what you like, and a player can be nervous in the extreme at the precise moment, or ice cold and calculating, but suddenly, unpractised, an almost 'accidental profundity' can invade his mind in a split-atom fraction of a second and he will do something he had never thought himself capable of had he planned it for a century.

The final word goes to Henry Wadsworth Longfellow in 'Tales of a Wayside Inn'. It reflects perfectly the relationship between Barry John and Llanelli Rugby Football Club.

> Ships that pass in the night, and speak to each other in passing,
> Only a signal shown and a distant voice in the darkness;
> So on the ocean of life we pass and speak to one another,
> Only a look and a voice; then darkness again and a silence.

18

Ieuan

The coach (1919 –2000)

Rugby Union referees are a breed apart. To anyone prepared to listen they will recount, in great detail, their exploits on the rugby field, explaining how they were single-handedly responsible for the superb standard of play at some match or other. Woe betide anyone, however, who dares to criticise the referee's performance. Ieuan Evans understood the mindset of the man with the whistle better than most and was not shy when an opinion was required. I can testify to this at first hand.

If there were a league table of less-than-acceptable displays by a referee, then that witnessed at St Helen's, in October 1974, in a fixture between Swansea and Pontypool would surely challenge for the top spot. The young referee in charge of the game that day was Alun Wyn Bevan. It was obvious from the kick-off that he wanted to impose his authority on proceedings, blowing his whistle at every opportunity to the detriment of a flowing game and much to the frustration of the players and supporters.

Minutes after the final whistle in the sanctuary of the referee's changing room, I was contemplating immediate retirement. Without warning the door flew open and there stood Ieuan Evans, the Swansea coach. 'That is the worst refereeing display I have ever seen,' he bellowed. 'If that's the best you can do, don't ever come here again.' With that he turned on his heel and slammed the door shut. While I dried off after a very, very long shower, I contemplated Ieuan's words and wondered how I could leave St Helen's without being seen!

As I emerged from the dressing room, you can imagine my surprise to find Ieuan awaiting my appearance. He insisted that I accompany him to the clubhouse, all the while warding off the abuse (vocal thankfully) from the home fans. That was Ieuan's way – he said what was on his mind, no more, no less and that was the end of the matter. He was not one to harbour a grudge.

While the name Ieuan Evans is immediately synonymous with the brilliant wing three-quarter who mesmerised us all during the 1980s and 1990s, it is the coach from Garnant in the Amman Valley who is fondly remembered as 'Ieuan'. He too was a master of his craft, a genius when it came to analysis and tactics. If there was a small flaw in his character, it was that Ieuan was always right – when it came to matters of rugby at least! What is more, he was not an establishment figure. He was forthright in his opinions and refused to toe the party line – a crime in a small country like ours! I am convinced that had Ieuan Evans been born a Kiwi or a Wallaby, then his many talents would have reaped their just rewards.

He was a great friend of Carwyn James' and often travelled to Italy when the former Llanelli coach lived there. He enjoyed success both at St Helen's and Stradey Park. His philosophy was that a rugby team was made up of fifteen players, and that each and every one should play a part in the success of that team. This success would embrace an entertaining, exciting approach for players and spectators alike. Although this strategy is commonplace enough in the modern game, during the 1960s and 1970s this was seen as something of a challenge and Ieuan Evans was compared with the great footballer Martin Peters – he was twenty years ahead of his time!

On a personal level, Ieuan was always sociable, a natural communicator and raconteur. His home, and where he felt most comfortable, was in the Welsh valleys. His father, Ianto 'Red' (an affectionate nickname suggesting his communist leanings) had instilled in the young Ieuan a sense of belonging and a sense of purpose in life.

His major contribution towards rugby success in Wales was with the game played at youth level. He was proud that such notables as Trevor Evans, Derek Quinnell, Phil Bennett and Terry Holmes had graduated to the highest level thanks to the country's youth infrastructure. Ieuan's entire rugby career was committed to nurturing youngsters and even when he reached lofty heights as Chairman of the Welsh Rugby Union, he never wavered from this commitment.

Although his love of rugby seemed all-encompassing, he did have two other great loves – his wife Renee and daughter Janet, an accomplished musician, linguist and latterly wine connoisseur, who recounts with affection the many happy times spent at Cowell Road in Garnant. Renee was his mainstay. It was she who brought another dimension to his life – rugby after all was not the be-all-and-end-all! Indeed, it had been ironic to see another side of him, in her company, as part of a group of bird watchers being instructed in the flora and fauna of certain localities! Little wonder that when Renee passed away, Ieuan seemed to lose his zest for life.

It seems that biographies appear in our bookstores on a daily basis recording the lives of some would-be celebrity or obscure pop star. Surely, it's time someone wrote a book about Ieuan.

Ieuan – as he was on the training field.

19
Llanelli 9   South Africa 10

A defeat to celebrate – with an ominous post-script

Every sporting enthusiast has his or her list of highlights. To some, this will include that occasion when their team won a major trophy; others, like myself, will treasure a singularly spectacular individual performance. In the same vein, I have friends who seem to spend most of their spare time at various concert halls being enthralled by the music of Mozart and Beethoven; others can be found roaming around art galleries captivated by the works of Rembrandt, van Gogh or Monet. What do we all have in common? For the crowds that flock to Glyndebourne, The Tate or Stradey Park, the answer is easy. It is the appreciation of talent in its most heightened form.

It was during the early 1970s that the Romanian tennis player Ilie Nastase was at the zenith of his career. Now, despite several visits to Wimbledon during this period and hours spent queuing at the turnstiles for a £6 ticket, I was never lucky enough to see him play. My admiration was always from a front-row seat in front of our small *Murphy* television set at home. Here was a true master at work, a combination of Brahms and Leonardo da Vinci. The tennis racquet appeared to be a natural extension of his arm while the ball was an object to be cajoled or smashed in turn. I'm not sure if Nastase had a game plan when he went out on court, but every now and again, he would suddenly produce a backhand, a volley or a lob, so audacious or so powerful that his opponent was left completely wrong-footed. The spectators in turn could only look on in awe.

Several column inches have been written over the years about Nastase's actions both on and off the court. To some commentators he was a genius, to others a clown. To say that he was a volatile character is something of an understatement. Many a linesman and umpire was subjected to his on-court histrionics, especially if he felt that he was the victim of a bad call.

Despite all this, Nastase was nothing if not an entertainer. His legendary late-evening doubles matches with Jimmy Connors are on a par with anything that Laurel and Hardy or Morecambe and Wise had to offer! Therefore, from a personal point of view, I would rank Ilie Nastase with such greats as Barry John, Johan Cruyff, Vivian Richards, George Best, Michael Jordan, Olga Korbut, Evonne Goolagong, Pele, Maradona, Sachin Tendulkar, Phil Bennett, Serge Blanco, Wayne Gretsky and Brian Lara. But what, I hear you ask, has Ilie Nastase to do with Stradey Park?

In an interview he gave Robert Philip of the *Daily Telegraph*, Nastase was asked to describe the one match, above all others, that had given him the most pleasure. Would it be the time that he won the US Open against Arthur Ashe in 1972? Or was it one of his performances in 1973, when he was victorious in 16 major competitions? Maybe it was that epic encounter against Bjorn Borg at Stockholm in 1975. In front of an extremely hostile and partisan crowd, Nastase beat the local hero in three straight sets – 6-2, 6-2, 6-1. Nastase's reply to the question was, however, quite unexpected.

The highlight of his career was the Wimbledon Final of 1972 when he played Stan Smith. The American won the match, and with it the Championship, in the twelfth game of the final set. Some tennis commentators have described this as one of the best men's finals ever played. The standard of tennis was exceptionally high with no quarter asked or given by either player. The lead changed hands throughout the match and the result was only decided in the last two games. As Nastase recalled the events of that day, he declared that for him tennis was an experience to be enjoyed by both players and spectators alike. In his opinion, players rely too much on power to win matches in the modern game; consequently, the elements of fun and finesse have disappeared.

If we were to translate Nastase's common-sense attitude and philosophy to rugby, then maybe the Llanelli stalwarts would rethink their view of the Llanelli vs Springboks fixture in January 1970. Perhaps we should occasionally take pride in a performance as much as in a favourable result. It was Dawie de Villiers's South Africans who were victorious, but the heroic display produced by all fifteen Llanelli players should not be underestimated.

The South Africans paid the Scarlets the ultimate compliment by fielding their strongest side, including star players Myburgh, Marais, Greyling, Ellis, de Klerk and du Preez. For two months before they embarked on the tour, the players had been ensconced at Stellenbosch University where they had been thoroughly prepared by the best South African coaches of the day. Little wonder, therefore, that the Scarlets were somewhat apprehensive before the match. Any pre-match worries were soon dispelled once the game got under way, however. The standard of rugby was exceptional with play flowing continuously back and forth from end to end. It seemed that no one wanted to kick the ball into touch.

The result was a fast, exciting, often breathtaking encounter. One such passage of play resulted in what was, arguably, the best try ever to have been scored at Stradey Park. The ball was passed amongst the Llanelli players with such abandon that some of the backs, centre John Thomas and outside half Gwyn Ashby in particular, found themselves involved in the play time and time again. Indeed the whole game, in its spririt of seemingly carefree abandon, was more reminiscent of beach touch-rugby on a Sunday-School outing! For their part the South Africans more than lived up to their reputation as one of the best teams in the world. Their defence was robust with many a bone-shattering tackle made on the men in scarlet. But Stuart Gallacher's team were equal to the task. By now the adrenaline, on and off the field, was flowing like lava down the slopes of Vesuvius as everyone sensed that something dramatic was about to take place. This came in the person of fullback Hamilton Jones who, just as he was about to be tackled, managed to release Alan Richards on the Llanelli right wing. As he raced towards the try-line, the noise from the excited crowd could be heard as far away as Loughor Bridge!

There have been many notable solo performances witnessed at Stradey Park over the years but this was undoubtedly one of the finest team performances. Clive John created a second try with a typical weaving run through the Springbok defence which resulted in prop Brian 'Bull' Butler crossing for a try with three opposition players clinging on his back. South Africa replied with two tries from Jan Ellis. It would be quite out of order to name a 'Man of the Match'. On this occasion thirty players could have been awarded bottles of champagne! The Llanelli team was as follows:

15 Hamilton Jones

14 Alan Richards

13 Graham Griffin

12 John Thomas

11 Roy Mathias

10 Gwyn Ashby

9 Gareth Thomas
Selwyn Williams (replacement)

1 Brian Butler

2 Arwyn Reynolds

3 Byron Gale

4 Stuart Gallacher (captain)

5 Derek Quinnell

6 Clive John

8 Hefin Jenkins

7 Alan John

Referee: Frank Lovis

Post script

The Llanelli coach at this time was Carwyn James. While the thousands of supporters at Stradey Park were urging on their team, Carwyn was on his way home to Cefneithin. Like many others, Carwyn was vehemently opposed to the apartheid system that was in place in South Africa. He had done his job by preparing the team, but his political beliefs would not allow him to take part in the day's events.

The irony of the situation was that Llanelli and the surrounding valleys were the bedrocks of industrialisation in South Wales. This was the home of the coal, steel and tin industries. This is where men lived and worked in conditions of real hardship. This is where unions were at their strongest; unions who fought for the rights of the individual. The irony of the situation was not lost on Carwyn James and it begs the question whether it was wise to invite a team from South Africa to Wales – and in particular to Llanelli – at the time.

A club game at Stradey featuring three heroes of that South African encounter: (from left to right) Stuart Gallacher, Alan John, and the versatile scrum half, Gareth Thomas.

20

Carwyn James

The Master

During the past 125 years, hundreds of players have represented Llanelli RFC, been proud to wear the scarlet jersey and then transferred to other clubs. There is, however, a small nucleus of players whose names will always be synonymous with the club. Whenever these names are mentioned, you immediately think of Llanelli. This select group would include Harry Bowen, Albert Jenkins, R.H. Williams, Ray Williams, Delme Thomas, Ray Gravell, Phil Bennett, Ieuan Evans, Gareth Jenkins and, of course, the late and great Carwyn James.

When Carwyn returned triumphantly from the Lions Tour of New Zealand in 1971, the world was his oyster. He could have coached great club and national teams the world over, such was the high esteem in which he was held. That he chose to remain faithful to Llanelli speaks volumes for the man.

Thousands of words have been written about Carwyn James, describing his many talents both on and off the rugby field. As well as being an exceptional coach, he was also a prolific writer and an eloquently astute broadcaster. Everyone who ever met him testifies to Carwyn's razor-sharp intellect, his extensive knowledge on a whole range of subjects and all agree that he was an exceptional human being. There is nothing that I could add which has not already been chronicled. However, I feel that a book about Stradey Park would be incomplete without some references to the master. What follows, therefore, are a few personal reflections.

During the 1970s and early 1980s, the highlight of my week came with the arrival on a Friday morning of *The Guardian.* I just couldn't wait to turn to Carwyn's weekly rugby column. This thousand-word literary gem was not merely an account of what had gone on before, or a prediction of what would be. This was an in-depth analysis of the state of the game, both locally, nationally and internationally. As one read through his thoughts, it was patently obvious how much research, analysis and forethought had gone into what he had to say. The articles were always interesting, sometimes amusing, and often thought-provoking and controversial in nature. Here was proof, if it were needed, of a master at his craft. I would like to quote a few examples:

> Rugby football is a player's game. He is the warrior who mattered in the primitive society; he takes the field, he does the actual thing, and he should have the qualities of honour, courage and pride in performance. Others; administrators, referees, coaches, scribes, are interpreters of the scene, but they should all observe the similar disciplines if they care for the game – to be interpreters and not mere describers, caring and not knocking, sensible rather than sensational. Such is not always the case.

*

> A young player must think and rethink his game many times over if he wants a first class career. If he does not, it will all be short, sharp and painful. To round up Dylan's lines: 'We shall see the boy of summer in his ruin'.

*

> I love an inner calm, a coolness, a detachment; a brilliance and insouciance which is devastating. Like Barry or Gerald. Some sniff the wind – they created it.

*

> We are breeding robots. We have few thinking players at the moment. The 80s promise little. Perhaps the drudge and the monotony of club training sessions, where everything is done by numbers, has numbed the brain to such an extent that it is incapable of original thought during an actual match. In some clubs, players are even ordered not to think. So no wonder they take the wrong options at critical moments.

Among many other outstanding qualities, I believe the one that singled Carwyn out from his peers was his inherent understanding of human nature. He had this ability to bring out the best in others and this was especially true of the rugby players who came under his tuition. There is much talk these days of the X-factor and Carwyn, I believe, possessed it in bucketloads. He could inspire, cajole, sympathise and empathise in equal measure with his players, and they in return rewarded him with 100% loyalty.

On the rugby field, his philosophy was that 'attack is the best form of defence' – a philosophy which is as pertinent in the modern game as it was in Carwyn's day and which is still in evidence at Stradey Park on a Saturday afternoon. This legacy would have made him a proud man.

I remember an interesting observation he once made during an address at Carmarthen Quins RFC during the club's centenary celebrations. He said that he often challenged players during his pre-match briefing. He invited them to make errors. I thought this a very strange statement but he then elaborated. 'By so doing', he said 'they will learn from these mistakes, learn how to perfect moves and as a consequence become more adventurous in their play. If players don't take chances, they don't succeed.' It's a pity that Sir Clive Woodward wasn't present in Carmarthen that evening!

He would always seek out the artistry in a player's performance. When he had such greats as Barry, Gerald, Gareth, J.P.R., David Duckham, John Taylor, Mike Gibson, and John Dawes in his cast, the task must have been a relatively simple one. It was just a matter of fine tuning before he got the desired level of performances and with them the results he craved.

Carwyn winning his first cap for Wales against Australia in 1958, alongside five fellow Scarlets.
Back row (left to right): Ray Williams, Cyril Davies, Wynne Evans.
Middle row (left to right): Carwyn James, Handel Rogers (WRU), R.H. Williams.
Front row: Terry Davies.

Some of Carwyn's philosophies were penned in an article he co-wrote with Tom Davies (BBC Sport) in the monthly magazine *Barn* which was published in 1971. The following is an extract in translation:

> Russia, along with other Communist countries boast of classless societies – everyone is deemed equal. The capitalist countries of the West on the other hand maintain that such a system is inoperable – that in any civilised society there has to be a system of hierarchy. Be that as it may, in the fullness of time, an evolutionary process will take place. Hopefully, this change will also be seen to occur within the realms of rugby union.
>
> Up until a year or so ago, a definite two-tier system was seen to operate within a fifteen-man rugby team. They could be segregated into 'the eight' and 'the seven'; 'the princes and the paupers', 'the chiefs and the warriors' – call them what you may but there was a definite fissure within a team. What each group called the other privately is not for publication, but it was obvious that one could not operate without the other. When a fifteen-man team ran out onto the rugby field, it was a fusion of two proud factions coming together to form one united whole.

If the spirit of adventure was paramount in Carwyn's plans, he was also on the lookout for a determination laced with stubbornness. These were the elements which made up his team. These qualities were demonstrated by the Australian captain Steve Waugh in the last test against England at the Oval in 2001. Despite a serious leg injury, Waugh scored an unbeaten 157 for his side while England's best batsman, Graham Thorpe, was permanently sidelined with minor ailments. I know which player Carwyn would have selected.

Carwyn was the architect of Llanelli's victory against the All Blacks in 1972. It is true to say that the Scarlets could have beaten a World XV or fifteen from Mars on that Tuesday afternoon, such was their standard of play. The squad had been meticulously prepared – tactically, psychologically and physically for the encounter and so it was no great surprise that they came away victorious. Carwyn James's vision and philosophy have been paramount in the many successes that have come Llanelli's way for the last 35 years. If Llanelli is the Manchester United of rugby football, then Carwyn is an amalgam of Sir Matt and Sir Alex.

21

The Centenary Year – a trilogy

i. Mr Rogers, a gentleman

According to the historical records, Llanelli RFC came into being on November 11, 1875, when a group of local gentlemen got together at the Athenaeum in town. If this is a true record, and there is no reason to doubt its authenticity, one then has to ask 'Why did the centenary celebrations take place in the season 1972/73?' Some cynics may conclude that it was to coincide with the visit of the New Zealand All Blacks! Be that as it may, the official celebrations coincided with the most successful season the club has enjoyed to date.

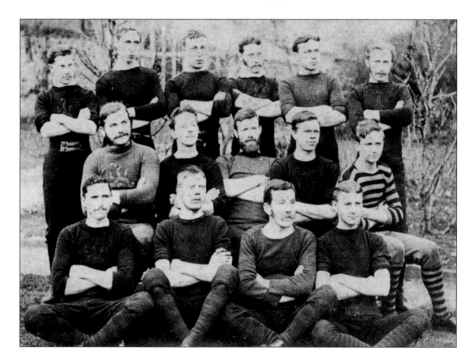

The captain, Delme Thomas, led his team to some historic victories. They beat Cardiff 30-7 in the Welsh Cup Competition, Swansea 6-4 in the Floodlight Alliance, and Newbridge 52-6 to win the Snelling Sevens. They also registered a resounding 33-17 victory against the Barbarians and a momentous win over the All Blacks (9-3). In passing, it should however be noted that one of the few teams to defeat the Scarlets that season were Hendy, of all people (18-16)! Hendy notwithstanding, it was a vintage year and all 600 guests who sat down to dinner in the marquee erected on the Stradey pitch were in celebratory mood as they enjoyed their champagne and caviar . . .

But to begin at the beginning, and that inaugural meeting at the Athenaeum. Records show that there were thirty people present, and it was decided that Mr Rogers, an influential industrialist of the period, would be invited to act as team captain. Mr Rogers was a former pupil of Rugby School, and it seems that his enthusiasm and wise counsel were decisive factors in his appointment. Another important issue was resolved at this first meeting – the club colours. These would be blue jerseys worn with blue caps!

Five games were played during that inaugural season – two against Swansea, two against Cambria (based in Swansea) and one against Carmarthen. When Mr Rogers was unavailable to captain the side, the task fell to two other notables, namely Mr Buchanan and Mr W.Y. Nevill (the latter being a member of a respected industrial and seafaring family in the town).

In a warm-up game played at the start of the season, some difficulties arose. It became impossible to differentiate between the two teams as their strip was identical! After some discussion it was decided that Mr Nevill's team would discard theirs! For the record, the bare-chested team won by a goal and a try to nil!

The first official match was played against Cambria on January 1, 1876. The result is an interesting one: the game was a draw but Llanelli were declared the victors. The laws of the game in those days were as inexplicable as the Duckworth-Lewis method of scoring in cricket today. Llanelli won because they had only grounded the ball defensively on one occasion, compared with four defensive actions from Cambria. Picture the headlines in the local press – 'Draw game – Llanelli win!' The second match, against Swansea, was played at Felinfoel and again the result was a draw. This time, however, both teams had two defensive touchdowns apiece and it was decided that the captain of each team would have to agree on the outcome of the match. In those days, if there was any doubt over a try or a score, the captains would have the final say.

Such a system would be a highly attractive proposition in the modern game. There would be no referees, no action replays and certainly no nonsense would take place around scrum, ruck, maul and line-out. If there was any disagreement during the game, this could be dealt with immediately after a reasoned debate between the two captains. It's as simple as that! Somehow I can't see Brian O'Driscoll and Tana Umaga agreeing!

And to younger readers, a reminder that Llanelli's double centenary celebrations should be staged during season 2075/76.

CLUB COLOURS:

1875 – 79	Blue jerseys and blue caps
1879 – 80	Blue and white jerseys
1881 – 83	Black jerseys with black and red stockings
1883 – 84	Rose and primrose jerseys
1884	Red jerseys with chocolate quarters
1884 – present:	Scarlet

ii. Mr Buchanan, the huntsman

If only Mr Buchanan had been an ornithologist and not a huntsman, he would be alive today; or at least he would have lived longer, a pair of binoculars being far less dangerous than a gun, after all! Arthur Buchanan hailed from London, was a banker by profession, worked at Marshfield during the day and enjoyed roaming the countryside during his spare time.

He was captain of Llanelli RFC from 1875 – 77, a rare honour when you consider that he had lived in the town for barely two years when he was elected. In that short time, he had thrown himself wholeheartedly into many of the town's activities. He was immensely popular, well respected and an enthusiastic leader of men. Considering these qualities, it is easy to see why he was chosen as team captain.

Three games were played in the 1876/77 season. The match against Swansea at St Helen's proved to be a close encounter, with the home team winning by a goal and a try to nil. Most of the play took place amongst the 24 forwards with the twelve redundant backs left to admire the view (there being eighteen players in each team at that time). The last game of the season was played on November 25 against Trinity College, Carmarthen. The result was a draw, but everyone agreed that had Mr Buchanan not been obstructed he would have scored the try which would have won the match for Llanelli. The captain had been hard done by and as a result the game disintegrated into total farce.

Nine days later Mr Buchanan was dead. As I noted at the beginning, the Llanelli captain enjoyed spending his leisure time roaming the countryside appreciating the wildlife. On that fateful morning of November 30, he left his lodgings at Greenfield Place and set forth with a group of friends who were out duck shooting. Whilst concentrating on the job in hand, he stumbled over a wall, lost his footing and inadvertently shot himself. He was 30 years of age. His loss was felt keenly by the whole town, as well as the rugby-playing community in Llanelli.

iii. The gentleman from Barbaria

Welsh people are often accused of being parochial, each little town and village having its own little dialect and turn of phrase. The rugby followers of the Gwendraeth, Tawe, Neath and Amman valleys will bear witness to this fact. If the home side are clearly outplaying the opposition, then it is not unusual to hear someone in the crowd shout out 'For goodness' sake boys, go back to Whitland/Llandeilo/Cardigan' – or whichever name was appropriate to that game. This was clearly a means of belittling the opposition.

The Scarlets have played host to the visiting Barbarians on two occasions. Once was during the 1960s when a packed Stradey Park saw Llanelli trounced by the opposition. The result was not the important issue on that night as the match was more of a celebration of the opening of the new changing rooms. It was also an opportunity for the fans to witness the rugby stars of the day in action.

The second visit by the historic Barbarians was in 1972 and came as part of the centenary celebrations. Carwyn James was the coach and he prepared his team as meticulously as he did for any important match. For him losing was not an option. By all means enter into the spirit of the occasion; yes, throw the ball around – but go out to win. The two teams on that day are listed below:

LLANELLI 33   BARBARIANS 17

Roger DAVIES	15	Ray CODD
Andy HILL	14	Viv JENKINS
Roy BERGIERS	13	Arthur LEWIS
Bernard THOMAS	12	Geoff EVANS
Ray GRAVELL	11	Lewis DICK
Phil BENNETT	10	Colin TELFER
Selwyn WILLIAMS	9	Ian McRAE
Adrian EVANS	01	Fran COTTON
Roy THOMAS	02	David BARRY
Tony CROCKER	03	Mike BURTON
Delme THOMAS	04	Peter LARTER
Derek QUINNELL	05	Chris RALSTON
Gareth JENKINS	06	Dai MORRIS
Hefin JENKINS	08	Andy RIPLEY
Barry LLEWELLYN	07	Feargus SLATTERY

Referee: Meirion JOSEPH (Cwmavon)

Scorers:

Roger Davies (2 tries)	Geoff Evans (try)
Andy Hill (try)	Lewis Dick (try)
Roy Bergiers (try)	Ian McRae (try)
Barry Llewellyn (try)	Ray Codd (1 pen.gl;
Phil Bennett (1 pen.gl; 5 conv.)	1 conv.)

In the company of a group of friends from Brynaman, I made my way to Stradey Park to watch the match. We were all Llanelli supporters but also keen to see the Barbarians play the style of rugby for which they are world famous.

In those days it was as much of an honour to be awarded a Barbarian shirt as it was an international cap e.g. Phil Bennett – Llanelli, Wales, British and Irish Lions and **Barbarians**.

The night was one to remember. The standard of rugby was of the highest order with both sides contributing to an extravaganza of rugby. However, as the match wore on, Llanelli were gaining the upper hand and a half-time score of 15-10 to the home side eventually became 33-17.

Ten minutes before the final whistle, the home side were in full flow when suddenly the Baa-baas started a counter attack from their own 25-yard line. Arthur Lewis started a run, carved through the home defence and made a dash towards the enclosure where we were standing. A simple pass to the wing three-quarter Lewis Dick and the Barbarians were in for a superb try. Unfortunately for the hapless Dick, he dropped the ball. From amongst the crowd came the familiar admonishment: 'Hey, mate. Go home to Barbaria!' It was at this point that even the referee, Meirion Joseph, was doubled up with laughter.

The Barbarians during one of their Easter tours in the early 1980s.
But which one of them once represented the Scarlets?

22

Delme

An inspiration in many ways

Do you know the answers to the following questions? Who is the only Llanelli player to have played in the front row of a British and Irish Lions test XV? Who is the second player from Bancyfelin to have worn the red shirt of his country? Who is the second player from Llanelli to have worn a Lions jersey in a test match before representing his country? Who is the first Llanelli player to have toured on three occasions with the British and Irish Lions? The answers: Delme, Delme, Delme and Delme.

Whenever a list is drawn up of the ten most famous players to have played for Llanelli RFC, the name Delme Thomas invariably appears in the top five. Delme was born in the Carmarthenshire village of Bancyfelin and for a period of some twenty years he faithfully made the fifteen-mile journey from his home village to Stradey Park to play for his beloved Scarlets.

Physically Delme was a giant of a man – tall, athletically built, possessing powerful, muscular arms. He was the ideal second-row forward and truly a master of his craft. He excelled at the line-out where his upper-body strength was such that he was able to outmanoeuvre the opposition either by his clean catching of the ball or by his deft tap-downs to his scrum half. That robust physique also made him a difficult adversary in other phases of the game: he was no mean scrummager and was often an immense presence at rucks and mauls. Indeed, his strength was always evident when a little extra effort was needed to push the opposition off the ball. In the maul, it was a pleasure to watch the way he wrenched the ball away from opposing forwards before releasing it into the safe hands of Selwyn or Gareth. For all his superhuman powers on the field, however, Delme Thomas was the gentlest, most reliable and highly respected person off it.

Delme gained 25 caps during his international career (the same number as Barry John, Haydn Tanner, Terry Holmes, Gwyn Travers and Norman Gale) but for him the pinnacle of his career came with the Llanelli victory over the New Zealand All Blacks in 1972. For all his trips abroad with the Lions and Wales, Delme was a home bird at heart, and his first loyalty was always to Llanelli RFC. To be chosen as captain for the club's centenary year was therefore to realise a dream and to face the All Blacks at Stradey Park was the proverbial icing on the cake.

Delme Thomas captained Llanelli on that dry but cloudy October day in 1972. With no health and safety regulations to comply with, Stradey Park was full to bursting point, the gates having been closed way before the appointed time for kick-off. Local factories had closed early to enable workers to attend the match; the typewriters in the offices around the town had fallen silent and there was a long line of Maxis, Marinas and Dolomites snaking their way to the ground. Someone was heard to comment that the only people who had been busy during the morning were the local GPs – they had been asked to sign hundreds of sick notes!

In the dressing room, the squad was ready for the fray. The coach, Carwyn James, had spent many a sleepless night preparing for the big day. Of course, both coach and captain were already familiar with the All Blacks' method of play, having spent the summer of '71 touring with the Lions. There was no need to study video tapes and have post-match analyses as is the current vogue. The strengths and weaknesses of the opposition were already well known to the Llanelli duo.

Carwyn had already briefed his team before they left the Ashburnham Hotel on the morning of the match. Therefore it was not deemed necessary to deliver another fiery ovation in the dressing room. Delme's words were simply 'We are wearing the Scarlet shirt, and we are representing our community, our town, our county and our country. We have a chance here of creating history.' How could one not respond to such a challenge?

No sooner had the captain finished what he had to say than Mike Titcombe, the referee, knocked at the door and invited the Llanelli players to follow Ian Kirkpatrick's All Blacks onto the field. The team left the sanctuary of the dressing room for the field which had now become a cauldron, bubbling with hope and expectation. What happened on that day has passed in to the annals of history. Delme Thomas's Llanelli, following his example and responding to his inspiration, beat the All Blacks.

This day may have been the zenith of Delme's rugby career, but there were also several occasions when a stroke of genius by the gentle giant resulted in a win for his team. One such event was the match at Murrayfield in 1971 between Scotland and Wales and, as Max Boyce would say, 'I was there!' The result was in doubt until the final minutes of the game and the Welsh supporters who had travelled north were very subdued. A line-out developed on the Scottish 25-yard line and as the home team had been awarded the throw in, it was expected that they would gain the advantage. It was then simply a matter of passing the ball to fly half, Jock Turner, who would presumably kick his team out of danger. If this had happened, then the result would have been a fair one even if it did mean Wales losing!

The visitors had scored the more tries, but Scotland had played attractive, adventurous rugby. The cliché that 'the game isn't over until the final whistle' was coined for occasions such as this.

As the ball was thrown into the line-out, Delme Thomas timed his jump to perfection and delivered the ball gift-wrapped to Gareth Edwards. The intention was obvious: get the ball out to Gerald Davies as quickly as possible. When the Llansaint wizard received the ball, there was a gap of approximately ten metres

The popular captain.

between the fleet-footed winger and the touchline. Panic had begun to infiltrate the Scottish defence. This was what Gerald relished. He approached fullback Ian Smith and then glided outwards in a parabola, and crossed for a splendid try. In our ecstatic thousands, we Welsh supporters leapt out of our seats in acclamation. This was comic-book stuff but there was even more gripping tension to come. The conversion was a difficult one, a yard or two in from the far touchline and it needed to succeed if the Welsh were to be victorious.

The responsibility of taking the kick was given to John Taylor, the London Welsh wing forward. This was a wise choice on the part of the captain John Dawes, as Taylor was a natural left-footed kicker. The whole of Murrayfield fell silent as the Welshman prepared to take the kick. As the brown-leather Gilbert rugby ball sailed through the uprights, the noise in the stadium reached a new climax and when seconds later referee Mike Titcombe drew proceedings to a close, a sea of red engulfed the jubilant Welsh players. In a sense it was a shame that one side had to lose. This had been such a keenly fought, close match that it was no surprise to see some of the Scottish players in tears as they left the field. Scotland 18 Wales 19.

The plaudits in the following days were all for John Taylor (or Basil Brush as he was fondly named by his team-mates). The play that had resulted in Gerald's try was soon forgotten. While no one would deny John Taylor his moment of glory, it is impossible to overestimate the contribution made by the two boys from Carmarthenshire – Gerald Davies and Delme Thomas.

Years from now, supporters of the game will continue to romanticize about the past and each will have his own opinion on individual players and individual matches. What they will all agree on, however, is the commitment, power, ability and dedication of one Delme Thomas, a role model in so many ways.

The match programme of Delme's finest hour.

23

D.Q.

The first 'Q' factor

For those of us born in the 1950s, the leter 'Q' is synonymous with the ink *Quink*, the porridge *Quaker Oats* and sometimes recalls some nightmarish encounters with the quadrilateral concept in geometry. For those teenagers of the 80s, it is the group Queen and the eccentric 'Q' of James Bond fame that equate with the seventeenth letter of the alphabet. Not so for the stalwarts at Stradey Park – for them there has only been, and will only be, one 'Q' and that is the former player and astute selector, Derek Quinnell.

Mr Quinnell, who hails from the Carmarthenshire village of Five Roads, is one of a select band of players who has played in a test match for the British Lions before making a debut for their own country – some others being Elvet Jones and Delme Thomas (both Scarlets), Bill Patterson, Elgan Rees and Brynmor Williams.

From the time that Derek burst onto the rugby scene at Llanelli, it was obvious that here was a player of exceptional talent and charisma with that extra quality that made him stand out from his peers. He was physically strong, determined, sometimes creative, sometimes destructive. His growing reputation caused some trepidation amongst his opponents, such that when visiting teams arrived at Stradey their first act was to check the team list. As soon as they came across the name 'Derek Quinnell' there were audible groans from the visitors' dressing room: 'Oh! no – he's playing.'

When the Lions touring party was announced in 1971, questions were asked in certain quarters regarding the wisdom of taking such an inexperienced youngster as Derek on such a gruelling trek. The Lions, after all, had never won a series in New Zealand, and there was no doubting the severity of the challenge ahead: a baptism of fire in no uncertain terms. Carwyn James, the Lions coach, was unmoved by such comments. If only Sir Clive Woodward had been blessed with such wisdom! Carwyn had every faith in his protegé having nurtured him during his early days at Stradey Park. There was also another crucial factor in his selection: Derek's ability to play in both the second and back rows.

Gabriel David and David Frost in their book *Lions' Share* marvel at how quickly the coaching team had managed to mould the players from the four home countries into such a strong, cohesive unit and in such a short space of time. It is also significant how often they praised the various contributions made by Gordon Brown, Ian McLaughlan, John Pullin, Peter Dixon, Sean Lynch and the rugged Derek Quinnell.

With the series tied at one win apiece, Carwyn James decided to blood Derek in the third test match. His brief was to shadow the influential All Black scrum half, Sid Going. In the second test match at Christchurch, Going, as unpredictable as a firework, had proved to be a driving force and was the catalyst of several scores. It was he who had controlled the game from the base of the scrum. His darting runs, especially on the blind side, had proved to be a real menace. With this in mind, the Cefneithin maestro decided that if the Lions had any real chance of winning the match, then they would have to negate Going's contribution. So it was that, on his debut test match in a Lions jersey, D.Q. found himself playing at No. 6 with instructions to 'Get Going!'

In the week leading up to the match, the training sessions provided opportunities for Derek to perfect his role in order to ensure that the All Black No. 9 would be outwitted. Ray Hopkins, one of only nineteen Lions players to appear in the four-test series and who later joined Llanelli, took on Going's role with Derek following him around the field like a terrier.

Derek scoring his only try for Wales – against Scotland in Cardiff, February 18, 1978.

The All Blacks were well and truly beaten in the match at Wellington. The forwards dominated up front; the half-backs Edwards and John controlled the tactical battle; Gerald Davies weaved his customary magic on the wing; and Sid Going, for once, was never in the game, having been effectively hustled, bustled and bullied by D.Q.

Flushed with success with the British Lions, Derek was eventually chosen to play for Wales. His first cap was as a replacement against France in 1972 – no one can can forget his spectacular entrance onto the field of play in the dying minutes to replace Mervyn Davies. When the signal came, Derek bounded from the tunnel area, brushed aside a bemused policeman and thundered onto the field of play. It is fair to say that this was his brother-in-law Barry John's last international match and it was only natural that Derek wanted to be part of the celebrations. Wales won the match by twenty points to six with Barry contributing four penalties.

As with most of the players in action on that day, Derek Quinnell's finest hour must have been that match at Stradey Park in October 1972. His enthusiasm, grit and sheer presence were very much in evidence on that historic occasion – as they were on many other red-letter rugby days. Did not Cliff Morgan breathlessly exclaim 'Brilliant by Quinnell!' as Derek put Gareth Edwards away for that much-replayed try for the Barbarians against New Zealand during the 1972/73 season? What then of the try he himself scored against Scotland in Cardiff in 1978? A try that I insist was almost mine! This was the season when Wales won the Triple Crown and the Grand Slam and I was fortunate enough to be one of the match officials serving as touch judge. It was also the winter when the landscape of south Wales had more than a passing resemblance to Siberia. There had to be something amiss when my fellow touch judge, Michael Rea, arrived home in Belfast days before I reached Brynaman!

To return to the try, Derek just pushed the Scottish No. 8 Alistair Biggar to one side, held the ball *à la* Michael Jordan in one hand, and ran menacingly towards the try-line. I was so carried away with the movement (being only two metres away) that I also ran hell for leather alongside him waiting for the pass!

To attain perfection in any sport is nigh on impossible, but in attempting to reach this state it is possible to scale great heights. Such a declaration could have been scripted specifically to describe the career of Derek Quinnell. He always strove for perfection and victory, always gave his all, as much to satisfy himself as to please others. To quote John Pesky, the former manager of the Boston Red Sox: 'People eat, sleep and perform better after a victory and even one's wife resembles Marilyn Monroe!'

24

Roy Bergiers

'The man of the moment'

There are certain moments which are indelibly imprinted in the memory, which never seem to fade with time. In the annals of sport the try scored by Roy Bergiers against the All Blacks on the October 31, 1972 is undoubtedly such an event. He was certainly the man of the moment on that unforgettable afternon.

I was there, together with some fifty children from Llandybie County Primary School, to witness the afternoon's proceedings. The children were seated on benches, squeezed in between the dead-ball line and the terrace. In theory we should have had an uninterrupted view of the game, but this did not prove to be the case. As soon as there was an exciting passage of play, the crowd in front of us jumped to their feet, completely obscuring the children's view. Fortunately, at six feet three-and-a-half inches, I was able to see some phases of the game and Roy Bergiers's try was one of them.

It was this try, to all intent and purpose, that sealed Llanelli's victory. Phil Bennett's penalty attempt hit the crossbar and rebounded straight into the arms of the New Zealand scrum half Lindsay Colling who was positioned between the try-line and the New Zealand 25-yard line. The Otago captain decided that his only course of action was to kick the ball into touch in the direction of the ground's Tanner Bank.

Whether or not he was aware of the fact at the time, Colling later learnt that Roy Bergiers was a former sprinter and his experience on the athletic track was now put to good use. As soon as the ball had left Phil Bennett's *Cotton Oxford* boot, Roy chased it like a true Olympian. Before Colling had time to put boot to ball, Bergiers was upon him, managed to charge down the kick, and get to the loose ball for the vital score.

It was a magnificent team effort on that historic afternoon, but one that had a special significance for one R.T.E. Bergiers – he was the one and only try scorer. Having watched a replay of the match on at least a hundred-and-one occasions, I can say with a degree of certainty that the hapless Colling (who sadly died of cancer in 2004) was in no way to blame for giving away the try. It was the pace, bravery and sheer determination of Roy Bergiers that won the day.

The centre-partnership he formed with Ray Gravell has since become part of Stradey legend. On the field, theirs was an almost telepathic understanding, each complementing the other in their styles of play. What is more, as is the way with centres, they were always looking out for each other.

Roy was to win his first international cap during that memorable season 1972/73 and this was against England at Twickenham. If the butterflies were evident before he ran onto the field, then any nerves were quickly dispelled thanks to the efforts of his team-mates J.P.R., Gerald, Gareth, Barry, Delme, Mervyn and Dai Morris. They made sure that the young Cardiff College of Education student settled into the game as quickly as possible. Roy was a powerful, skilful centre three-quarter who became a Boy's Own hero at Stradey Park. He varied his angles of running intelligently, always looking to release players in better, more threatening positions. Breaching defences, tearing upfield, involved in fingertip transfers . . . Roy Bergiers was a class act and an integral part of the highly successful Llanelli team of the Seventies.

Roy Bergiers representing West Wales (long before the days of regional rugby!) against New Zealand at St Helen's, Swansea, in 1978. Here he prepares to tackle his opposite number, Bill Osborne.

25
That Historic Scoreboard

WHERE ARE THEY NOW?

15 Roger DAVIES
Born and bred in Dafen, Llanelli. In the latter stages of his playing career via
Maesteg he rejoined Swansea where he became an assistant coach to Mike
Ruddock in the early Nineties. Currently a deputy headteacher at Pentrechwith
Primary School in the city.

14 J.J. WILIAMS
A native of Nantyffyllon and now a successful businessman in Mid
Glamorgan. Won 30 caps for Wales and toured with the British Lions in 1974
and 1977. His son Rhys, a talented 400m hurdler, recently represented Britain
in the world championships in Helsinki.

13 Roy BERGIERS
A retired Physical Education teacher who lives in his native Carmarthen.
Scored the only try in the game. Won 11 caps for Wales and toured South
Africa with the British Lions in 1974.

12 Ray GRAVELL
Currently enjoying a renaissance in his career as an actor, presenter and
commentator. Won 23 caps for his country and toured South Africa with the
British Lions in 1980.

11 Andy HILL
Hails from St Thomas in Swansea. Moved from Gorseinon Rugby Club to
play at Stradey thanks to the influence of Norman Gale's father. Scored 310
tries for Llanelli; played once for Wales 'B' against France when he kicked a
penalty goal to win the game. Lives near Fforestfach.

10 Phil BENNETT
Lives in Felinfoel and works for Carmarthenshire County Council as a Sports
Development Officer. Won 29 caps for his country, man of the series with the
British Lions in South Africa in 1974 and team captain in New Zealand in 1977.
Also works as a respected and astute rugby pundit on television and radio.

9 Ray HOPKINS

Affectionately known as 'Chico', he moved from his native Maesteg to play for Llanelli before changing codes to play for Swinton. Replaced Gareth Edwards twice – at Twickenham in 1970 when he scored a vital try in a 17-13 victory and for the British Lions in Dunedin in 1971 when John Dawes's men won by 9-3. Now an antiques dealer.

1 Barry LLEWELLYN

A successful businessman in Pembrokeshire living in Saundersfoot. Won 13 caps for Wales. Rugby just one of his many other sporting interests.

2 Roy THOMAS

Known to rugby fans from Penclawdd to Pontypridd as 'Shunto'. Very unlucky to miss out on a Welsh cap. Recognised throughout England and Wales as a truly great player. Now enjoying retirement and living in Loughor.

3 Tony CROCKER

Continues to live and work in Llanelli. A regular visitor to Stradey where he played until his retirement in 1976. A truly great front-row forward who these days would have been a regular in the red shirt of Wales.

4 Delme THOMAS

The winning captain. Won 25 caps for Wales and toured with the British Lions in 1966, 1968 and 1971. Great player; great man.

5 Derek QUINNELL

Another successful businessman who continues to live and work in the Llanelli area. Played in a test match for the British Lions in 1971 before winning a cap for Wales.

6 Tom DAVID

Joined from Pontypridd shortly before the match against New Zealand. A popular figure at Stradey before he returned to Sardis Road in 1976. Won 4 Welsh caps and toured South Africa with the Lions in 1974.

8 Hefin JENKINS

Born and bred in Burry Port and continues to have a close association with the club as one of its heritage directors. A Surveyor with the Abbey Building Society. Hefin should have been born in another country – he would have been a regular inernational.

7 Gareth JENKINS

The current club coach who has also been involved with both the Wales and British Lions squads. A cornerstone of Llanelli and the Scarlets. Toured Japan with the Welsh team in 1975; a serious leg injury resulted in his premature retirement.

The Immortal Victors.

Back row: Selwyn Williams, Phil Bennett, Tom David, Tony Crocker, Derek Quinnell, Barry Llewellyn, Gareth Jenkins, Ray Gravell, Hefin Jenkins, Roy Thomas, Alan James, Chris Charles, Brian Llewellyn.

Front row: Gwyn Ashby, Bert Peel, Roger Davies, Andy Hill, Roy Bergiers, Norman Gale, Delme Thomas (captain), Carwyn James, J.J. Williams, Ray Hopkins, Meirion Davies.

26

Barry Llewellyn

'Nice and easy does it . . .'

It was almost nine o'clock in the evening when a very tired Alun Morris Jones and I arrived at the impressive Central Hotel in Auckland. We had spent the day filming in Rotorua and Lake Taupo and were keen to have a shower, a bite to eat and then crash into our respective beds. Unfortunately for us, we couldn't park anywhere near our hotel as the whole area was taken over by outside-broadcast units from the New Zealand Broadcasting Corporation.

When we eventually arrived at the reception desk, we were told that a live transmission was taking place from one of the main conference rooms. The occasion was the eightieth birthday of the mountaineer, climber and sometime bee-keeper, Sir Edmund Hillary, who was being honoured by his fellow countrymen that very evening.

After completing our registration cards, Alun and I made our way to our room to watch the final stages of the event on our television screen. Sir Edmund was presented with a cut-glass decanter, commemorating his many achievements, and then with tears in his eyes he rose to say a few words of thanks. What he said in those brief moments made a lasting impression on me.

> I started university with great intentions but failed to complete the course. I then decided to concentrate on my interests and as a result received six doctorates from some of the world's foremost universities.

In his early teens, Edmund Hillary spent most of his time helping his father with the business of bee-keeping. It was a physically taxing profession, but as the work was seasonal, this left the young Hillary with some spare time in which to pursue other interests. He loved the outdoor life and spent a great deal of time walking in the mountains of South Island where his interest in moutaineering developed. It wasn't long before he left the comparative safety of his native mountains and ventured further afield where new challenges presented themselves. The culmination of these of course came when he and his Nepalese sherpa, Tenzing Norgay, conquered the world's highest mountain, Everest, on May 29, 1953.

What is the connection between Sir Edmund Hillary and Barry Llewellyn? The latter was no mountaineer, although physically he could be described as a mountain of a man. Born and brought up in Llanelli, Barry was the son of a local businessman. His father, Bryn, who hailed from Gwauncaegurwen, was the owner of a small colliery in Glanaman producing high quality anthracite coal.

Barry received his early education at Llanelli Grammar School before moving on to Loughborough College to study Physical Education. From here he went on to train as a teacher at Caerleon College of Education, completing his studies in 1969. It was during these student years that Barry first played for Llanelli. This realised a boyhood dream but he decided to remain true to his college side and continued playing for Caerleon throughout the 1967/68 season. He enjoyed playing at No. 8, even though his natural position was prop forward. He was also the first-choice goal-kicker for his team and contributed 180 points in that capacity.

At the beginning of the 1968/69 season, Barry received a telephone call from Nick Carter, the highly respected secretary of Newport Rugby Club, asking him to play for the Black and Ambers. Follwing a tragic road accident, involving the club captain Martin Webber, the team was left without a loose-head prop forward. The college authorities consented and so it was that for the rest of the season Barry Llewellyn was seen playing at Rodney Parade in the black-and-amber strip of Newport.

His performances were such that the invitation to tour Australia and New Zealand with the Welsh squad came as no surprise. A few days before the team was due to leave, Barry insisted on playing for the college in their final match of the season against Caerphilly at Virginia Park. This was typical of the man: on Wednesday afternoons he would turn out for the college and then travel to Rodney Parade in the evening for a training session. In the opening minutes of the game, scrum half Billy James suffered an injury which forced him from the field of play. In those days, replacements were only allowed at international level, which is why D. B. Llewellyn found himself at scrum half for the remainder of the game – a performance which earned much praise from his half-back partner, Gethin Thomas.

So, what links the bee-keeper's son from New Zealand with that of the colliery owner's son from South Wales? I suggest that it was their rejection of convention and the commonplace. They were both free spirits. Conforming was anathema to both. For Barry, the freedom to come and go as he pleased was of paramount importance. And nothing illustrates this more clearly than his declining of the invitation to join the Lions tour of Australia and New Zealand in 1971. Much as he enjoyed playing rugby, the thought of spending months away from home, bending to the constraints and obligations of an organised tour, was not an option. He much preferred to spend his time pursuing his other interests, which included hunting, fishing, sailing and surfing. He subsequently developed business interests also, very much a chip off the old block, and now owns a succession of outlets, both around Tenby and abroad.

On the rugby field he was a giant. He was a destructive runner, powerful enough to hold his own in most situations. However, it was in the line-out that he came into his own. If you can imagine a young bull released from its pen and thundering out into the bullring to challenge the matador – then you have a clear vision of Barry Llewellyn's impact from a line-out! As soon as the ball was released from the hooker's hand, Barry would race to the back of the line to receive the tap down and in so doing completely annihilate the opposition. He had boundless energy, was fleet of foot and a natural footballer. To see him draw his opponent and then release the ball was to witness artistic execution, all the more admirable when you consider that this was done by a six-foot-three, eighteen-stone forward.

Barry's many talents on the rugby field enabled him to play in more than one position, as illustrated by his selection at open-side wing forward for Llanelli in the Schweppes Cup Final victory against Aberavon in 1974. The early 1970s proved memorable in Barry's rugby career. The pinnacle, of course, was the victory against the All Blacks at Stradey Park, but it must be remembered that Barry and Delme were Llanelli's only representatives in the magnificent Wales 1970/71 Grand Slam team.

There are many rugby pundits who would argue that Barry Llewellyn was one of the best rugby forwards of his generation, both at club and international level. Of these, several were New Zealand journalists who lauded his performances during the 1969 tour to the Land of the White Cloud. For those aficionados who regularly meet to analyse the long line of great players who have represented Llanelli, most would list Barry in the best XV of all time. How would he rate under the present professional structure? The answer is simple. He would be playing for Hendy (where he started his career) or Tenby – he would be playing purely for pleasure. Not for Barry the constant training sessions, the post-match video analysis, the continuous travel armed with the latest i-pods and Play Stations to while away the tedium. Not that he was a rebel; more a realist.

Barry Llewellyn about to peel off the line-out – one of his characteristic ploys.

27

Phil Bennett

Duende

There is a word in Spanish which is used when other superlatives are deemed inadequate. *Duende* has no equivalent in English or Welsh but it accurately describes that doyen of Welsh rugby, Phil (or Philip as his wife Pat likes to call him) Bennett. He was a rugby player whose talents defy definition; a mercurial mix of the impressive, the unexpected and – dare I say it – the superhuman.

Duende might also describe Cliff, Bleddyn, Barry, Gerald, Gareth, Ieuan, Jonathan and Shane – that elite group of players who, like the great Welsh poets, can be identified solely by their Christian names. But for all their genius, it is Phil, the Llanelli, Wales and British Lions outside half, that many would place at the head of this group.

All over the rugby-playing world, in clubhouses and bars, there is always a debate raging regarding the respective strengths and weaknesses of the best players, past and present. Inevitably, the hottest subject under review is the outside half position, and in Wales, we have over the years been proud of those players who have donned our No, 10 shirt.

For the older generation, Cliff Jones who hailed from Pont-y-clun would head the list of greats. Surely his try for Wales against Scotland at Cardiff Arms Park in 1934 was one of the best ever scored. Others would argue that Cliff Morgan and Jackie Kyle should be awarded the top accolade. In later years we have borne witness to the master-class performances of Barry John, Hugo Porta, Mark Ella, Michael Lynagh, Carlos Spencer, Daniel Carter and, of course, Phil Bennett.

From time to time, it has to be acknowledged that it is the kicking expertise of the fly half that wins the day. Jonny Wilkinson, Neil Jenkins, Grant Fox, Diego Dominguez and Andrew Mehrtens are testimony to this fact with some heart-stopping exhibitions of accurate goal-kicking. Playing at outside half, however, is not just about being able to kick on a sixpence – it needs the card-shuffling skill of a Paul Daniels; the self-discipline of an Ayrton Senna guiding his car around a circuit at breakneck speed; the technique, style and creativity of a fashion designer such as Armani; the classical stroke play of a Lara or Tendulkar; the unique vocal talent of a Bryn Terfel and the vision and attention to detail of great architects like the two Franks, Gehry and Lloyd Wright. And one thing is certain: Phil Bennett possessed these, and other, qualities in abundance. Suffice it to say that he is one of the best outside halves and footballers ever to have played the game.

The master kicker.

I first saw Phil's genius at work during the mid-Sixties. The occasion was the Llanelli Schools' Sevens held at Stradey Park. He was playing in the Under 15 section representing Coleshill School. This competition was not only supported by local schools, but thanks to the hard work and foresight of the teachers in the area, it attracted competitors from all over Britain. Both state and public schools sent representatives so that every Easter all roads led to Stradey Park.

I was sitting in the main stand and eagerly anticipating the next match involving Amman Valley Grammar School. What happened before my very eyes in the following moments left me, and the few thousand spectators present, completely spellbound. The young lad put on a display of breathtaking audacity which left us all mesmerised – the sidesteps, the ghostly running and the incredible pace were all in evidence.

It is often said that it is the speed over the first ten yards which is important in a rugby player's armoury. This is often what separates the genius from the ordinary player. Scores of rugby players can be seen every weekend who, through commitment and dedication, have managed to satisfy the necessary criteria and play at the highest level. However, there is a small nucleus whose talents exceed those of their peers. Phil Bennett is one such player – his was a unique talent. It is true that he was quick over the first ten yards but he was also extremely quick off the mark, especially so when the ground was hard and dry. The comparisons with a bullet from a gun, or a greyhound from its trap really are fair ones. This made him nigh-on impossible to tackle. He left his opponents standing and the adoring fans in raptures.

There are several cameo performances about which to reminisce. One scene is the second test match at Pretoria in 1974. The British Lions outside half took full advantage of ground conditions and ran like an Olympic athlete towards the South African try-line. His sidestepping moves to avoid the opposing defence would have made Torvill and Dean proud. Indeed it seemed as if the graceful Mr Bennett was himself skating along on ice, leaving all and sundry prostrate in his wake.

Another much-talked-of try is the one scored against Scotland at Murrayfield in 1977. This was truly a team effort (instigated by Gerald Davies) with Phil again causing mayhem amongst the Scottish defence before launching himself over the try-line right undeneath the uprights. Whether he was the instigator or the executioner of a score, Phil was a master craftsman.

The try scored by Gareth Edwards at Cardiff in 1973, when the Barbarians took on the mighty All Blacks, will go down in posterity as one of the finest tries ever scored. Edwards, Quinnell, David, Dawes, Pullin and J.P.R. were all involved in the movement of the millennia. But who was it who got the ball rolling as it were? It was the maestro from Felinfoel. He took possession running backwards and, under enormous pressure, decided to attack. The rest, as they say, is history. Gareth Edwards is credited with scoring the try, but it was all set in motion by Phil Bennett.

My favourite is the try scored at Stradey Park one bleak Wednesday night towards the latter part of the 1970s. The opposition that night was Newport, and Phil was playing at fullback. He seemed to relish the freedom of the open spaces afforded him in this position, resembling at times a lone huntsman stalking the Kalahari. From time to time, however, flashes of genius appeared and a defensive move would suddenly be transformed into one of glorious attack. Phil accepted a pass near his own 25-yard line and proceeded to run back towards his own goal line. He then suddenly changed direction, sidestepped a few desperate opponents, glided some ten metres downfield perilously skimming the touch line, veered inside and made his way towards centre field. Then, just as suddenly he again changed the course of his run, sprinting along the touch-line and crossed the try-line. The Newport players could only stand in awe, their attempts at tackling this apparition had been futile. I was the referee that evening and, together with the five thousand other supporters present, realised that the effort would be forever etched in the memory.

1977 promised to be a good year for Phil. He was awarded the ultimate accolade of captaining the British and Irish Lions on their New Zealand tour. However, the dream became a nightmare as the Lions narrowly lost the series. Although the weather conditions during the tour had been atrocious with heavy rain being the order of the day, the Lions forwards had dominated the New Zealand eight. Unfortunately, the backs were unable to capitalise on this possession and for this reason, Phil, as captain, came in for a great deal of criticism from supporters and press alike. The tour proved to be an unhappy one with the coach, John Dawes, sadly unable to inspire his squad.

Phil Bennett weaving his magic at Stradey

However, once back on home soil, Phil regained his composure and confidence. He was helped by his close friends and many hours representing Felinfoel on the cricket field. The following season saw him leading Wales to a Grand Slam. England were defeated by nine points to eight at Twickenham, Scotland were crushed at Cardiff and Ireland yielded to the marauding Welsh in Dublin. The final hurdle was the home game against France. With the *tricolores* leading by 7-0, the outside half took matters into his own hands by scoring a try in the corner. This was soon followed by a second try when he took advantage of an inside pass from club colleague, J.J. Williams. At the end of the match, it was announced that this was to be the last international for both Gareth Edwards and Phil Bennett. What a way to bow out from the game at its highest level!

Nowadays, Phil is a regular summariser on both BBC radio and television. His opinions are always forthright, balanced and fair which makes him as respected a pundit as he was a player. He is a role model for any young player and as such it would be appropriate if the Board of Directors saw fit to name one of the stands at the new stadium in his honour. Phil Bennett – superstar!

Phil with the WRU Challenge Cup that the Scarlets made their own in the 1970s.

Phil being forced to listen to another of Ray Gravell's Stradey stories!

28

Allt-y-grug Mountain

A true story

The following event could only have taken place at Stradey Park. Certainly not at St Helen's, Sardis Road or the Gnoll. This is because Stradey Park is frequented by a certain kind of supporter. One-eyed? Maybe. Verbose? Frequently. Fair-minded? Occasionally. Amusing? Always! And this kind of supporter is never shy of passing comment on all that occurs – on or off the field.

The incident in question is not chronicled in any official document. It will not be found in the National Library of Wales at Aberystwyth or in the archives of Carmarthenshire County Council. No mention was made of it in the local press or in *The Western Mail*. Unfortunately the journalists present were non-Welsh speakers and were therefore excluded from the general hilarity which resulted after the incident.

For my part, the events of the evening have become somewhat clouded in the mists of time. I cannot recall with any great certainty in which month the match took place, who the teams involved were or what colour strips they played in. I do remember that it was a charity match and that several past and present international stars had been persuaded to take part. As was usual in that period, the supporters turned out in droves to see the big names of Welsh sport and to enjoy what was to be an extravaganza of open rugby. It is interesting to note at this point that the only international player who never appeared at these events was J.P.R. Williams. It was not that he disapproved of such encounters, merely that the organizers could not take the risk of including him in the starting line-up! J.P.R. played every game with a 110% commitment – he could not differentiate between a 'friendly' and an international game against France. Poor old Garth Morgan, the Brynaman wing three-quarter, would receive the same treatment as Jean François Gourdon, the French flyer.

As far as I can recall, the two teams were made up of players representing Llanelli and Swansea against a combined Neath and Aberavon team. Stradey Park was almost full to capacity and the thousands present were in carnival mood. At this point I should provide a little background information. During this period, the mountain dominating the villages of Ynysmeudwy and Godre'r Graig in the Swansea Valley was constantly in the news. After several weeks of heavy rainfall, there had been several mud-slides, resulting in the closure of the main road through the villages and the evacuation of several houses. The officers of Lliw Valley District Council were constantly monitoring the situation and daily bulletins were issued on the subject of 'Allt-y-Grug – the moving mountain'.

91

But to the match in question. One of the forwards representing the Neath and Aberavon XV was the second-row forward, and 'man mountain', Brian Thomas. In his heyday Brian had played for Cambridge University, Neath and Wales. He was one of the most fearsome forwards ever to don the Welsh shirt, and at 17 stones, his French counterparts had dubbed him *trés formidable*. He was the player you chose to have in your team not in the opposing side. Now that he had retired from the game, Brian had added considerably to his already imposing bulk – so much so that he found it rather difficult to keep up with the play.

With twenty minutes remaining of an open and attractive encounter, one of the Stradey faithful suddenly realised that the former star was not contributing much to the action. In fact, he seemed to be crawling at snail's pace from one line-out to the next. Without a thought for his future safety, an anonymous voice was heard to shout out, 'Brian, hurry up. There's a mountain in Godre'r Graig moving faster than you!'

29
Grav

West is best!

Proud, sincere, honest – just some of the qualities attributed to Ray Gravell, the gentle giant from Mynydd y Garreg near Cydweli. It is true to say that this quiet village in the Gwendraeth Valley is Ray's *nirvana*. This is where he was born and brought up, and this is where he and Mari intend spending the rest of their days.

If Mynydd y Garreg is his physical home, then undoubtedly Stradey Park is his spiritual one. It was here as a young child that he was brought to watch the Scarlets play (from the safety of the Tanner Bank) by his father who was a faithful Scarlet supporter. It was here, also, that Ray was to enjoy a very successful career as a player, and latterly as a fanatical supporter and respected President of the club.

Swerving on the outside – once again!

Thousands of words, in articles and books, have been written about the 'exocet from West Wales'. 'West is best' has always been Ray's philosophy, but despite his obvious commitment to Llanelli Rugby Football Club, Ray is held in high esteem throughout the rugby-playing community.

It is quite an emotional experience travelling around the world in his company. Wherever we happen to be, whether it is Limerick, Hawick, Bath, Perpignan, Mendoza, Durban or Rotorua, he is immediately recognised and greeted as an old friend. People will cross the street just to shake his hand, and they will all be accorded the same degree of politeness and warmheartedness that we have come to know and love about him. With Ray Gravell, what you see is genuinely what you get.

Inevitably in any discussion about the modern game, we tend to talk about centres like Brian O'Driscoll, Philippe Sella, Tim Horan, Jeremy Guscott and Tana Umaga, omitting to mention the giants of the past. Believe me, Ray Gravell was one such player. Though a crash-ball centre to many, he could also be creative when necessary. Indeed the fact that his two wingers, J.J. Williams and Andy Hill, scored so many tries bears testimony to this.

That Ray was labelled a 'crash-ball' centre at all had as much to do with his robust physique as his manner of play. It is true to say that he would have struck fear into the heart of anyone who met him in a dark alley near the North Dock of a Saturday night. Ray attributes this solid musculature to some quality genes and his mother's wholesome cooking! Not for him the body-building regime associated with hours in the gym, or on the dunes or any other method currently in vogue.

From the Seventies onwards, the Scarlet philosophy was to move the ball around the park and especially along the back line at every opportunity. With the genius that was Phil Bennett playing at outside half, this proved to be a winning formula. One of Phil's great attributes was his phenomonal speed. His ability to make a searing break and completely wrong-foot the opposition was legendary. Aided as he was by the other thoroughbreds, the Llanelli try-count kept on soaring.

Opposition defences were constantly in a state of disarray, hypnotised by the astute angles and patterns of play of those jack-in-the-box attackers. However, there were occasions when Llanelli did not have it all their own way. Some defences were better organised than others – and this is when Ray and his fellow centre, Roy Bergiers, came into their own. This was the time when a quick ruck was called for, when it was necessary to regain the ball and then create the space for a counter attack. And Ray was a master of the art of hurtling his body at his opponent. This earned him a reputation as a hard player – a trait completely at odds with his true character.

An interesting incident took place at the Parc des Princes during a match between France and Wales. Ray found himself at the bottom of a ruck and staring into the blazing eyes of the garlic-scented 'Desperate Dan' himself – none other than the French No. 8, Jean-Luc Joinel. For some reason best known to himself, Ray grabbed the player by the throat and started shouting 'Froggie! Froggie! Froggie!' Now provoking Jean-Luc was not considered a sensible course of action. But before the formidable Frenchman had time to respond, in speech or action, Grav just smiled meekly and said, 'Joking, only joking!'

Five minutes later, as he was regaining his feet after yet another bone-crunching tackle, Ray was suddenly felled by a right hook to rival Muhammad Ali's. With blood pouring from his nose and stars circling his eyes, Grav was immediately rescued by the first-aid man wielding his magic sponge. In the middle of the ensuing pandemonium, Monsieur Joinel leaned over Grav and with a big grin on his face uttered the immortal words, 'Joking, only joking!'

His previous visit to the same stadium in 1975 was for his first international cap. The ouside half on that day was John Bevan. His style of play was completely different from that of Phil Bennett. Bevan was always looking for a half break from a set piece. He would be subject to the inevitable tackle from his opposite number, but in so doing often managed to release the ball to a supporting player. And at Bevan's shoulder, Grav showed his critics that not only could he assume the role of juggernaut when that was required, but that he could also display the light-footed finesse of a ballet dancer.

To see him with ball in hand dancing through the French defence before timing his pass to the micro-second was a lesson in centre three-quarter play to any aspiring schoolboy. Wales's shock victory over France that day was due in no small part to the Welsh centre's supreme efforts.

Scores of Ray's fellow players will testify to Ray's warm-hearted, engaging personality. His friends, however, will also be aware of his lack of self-confidence, on and off the rugby field. I remember several occasions during the 1970s when I happened to officiate at matches involving the Scarlets. As is usual before the teams take to the field, it is the referee's responsibility to visit the changing rooms and check the players' studs. It was while I was in the process of so doing that I was suddenly grabbed, literally by the throat, by Mr Gravell and challenged 'Who is the best centre in Wales?' 'Why, you Ray' was my immediate (and judicious) response. Somewhat startled, I was then assured that this was the weekly ritual that Grav had to perform to prepare himself psychologically for the ensuing encounter.

One anecdote perfectly illustrates Ray's pre-match preparations. The rugby season was drawing to its close, and Llanelli and Bridgend were competing for the top slot in *The Western Mail*'s unofficial championship table. Ray was pacing around the visitors' dressing room at the Brewery Field like a caged lion, while the same questions were again and again asked of his team-mates: 'Who's the most creative centre in Wales?' 'Who is the most attractive player in world rugby?' 'J.J., who's the most destructive centre in rugby history?' Again the answers were the same – 'You, Ray!'

Some ten minutes into the game, a scrum formed on the halfway line, and the ball shot out into Ray's hands. Spying the tiniest of openings between Steve Fenwick and Lyndon Thomas, Grav shot through the two Bridgend defenders like a bat out of hell. He then raced downfield for some 30 metres, drew his opponent and passed the ball skilfully to the supporting J.J. Williams. With just 15 metres to sprint to the try-line, a Llanelli score was inevitable. Unfortunately for the Scarlets, they had not reckoned on the speedy response of Bridgend's J.P.R. Williams. The fullback's immense physical presence and his ability to cause grown men to tremble after one of his bone-shuddering tackles were legendary. But he was also fleet of foot and like a tiger chasing its prey, he launched himself at J.J., bringing him to ground just inches short of the try-line.

It was obvious that poor J.J. Williams was in a great deal of pain as a result of the encounter. First on the scene was Raymond Gravell. 'Quick, Ray. Get Bert Peel. I'm in severe pain. I think I might have broken my collar bone.' The reply was a little unusual and not the one the injured winger was expecting to hear. 'Yes, yes, yes J.J. All in good time. But who's the best centre in Wales?'

Ray Gravell – a fighter to the core. A Welshman to the core.

30

J. J.

Flair, finesse and a fair amount of panache

There are times when a sporting incident takes one's breath away, causes the heart to skip a beat; a moment of such high drama as to be forever etched in the memory. A moment when we can sing in chorus with Max Boyce – 'I was there!' Two such occasions were witnessed during the last weekend of the Athens Olympic Games.

The first was when a 30-year-old middle-distance runner from Kent, who had spent years overcoming many obstacles, won sport's most prestigious prize twice over. She was Kelly Holmes, double Olympic gold medallist. The second was the final of the 4x100-metre relay event for men, when the British team against all expectations, also won gold. In the days leading up to the final Saturday, the men's relay team had endured a barrage of criticism from commentators (such as Michael Johnson and Colin Jackson) and supporters alike. The consensus was that the team was underperforming; that they lacked commitment, and that despite all the time and money lavished on them, there was little hope that they would return home as medallists.

Indeed, relations between the two camps reached an all-time low when Johnson went as far as to suggest that Darren Campbell had feigned injury in one of his preliminary heats. Thus, on the morning of the final, it would have been a brave man who would put any money on the British team standing on the winners' rostrum at the close of the day. After all, the last time Britain won the event was in Stockholm in 1912 (the USA having won on 15 occasions since that time).

Whatever inspired Campbell, Gardener, Devonish and Lewis-Francis on that day in Athens, only they will ever know. Perhaps it was the sting of the criticism levelled at them in the press or maybe it was the words of Nelson Mandela: 'Sport has the power to change the world, the power to inspire, the power to unite people in a way that little else can.' Nevertheless, the preparations beforehand were intense, with every detail checked and rechecked.

The team took to the track with a determination which had hitherto been lacking. They were out to prove their critics wrong, and to regain some degree of that self-respect which had been seriously undermined in the preceding days. Whatever the source of the inspiration, the quartet gave the performance of a lifetime. Every bone, muscle and sinew in their bodies was tested to the ultimate degree on that track in Athens and for it they achieved the ultimate accolade.

Those elements of determination and the will to succeed are also part of the genetic make-up of the wing three-quarter from the Llynfi Valley, J.J. Williams. Let us not forget that J.J. himself was a successful athlete before he embarked on his rugby career, having represented Wales in the Commonwealth Games in Edinburgh in 1970. How gratifying it must have been for him, therefore, to see his son, Rhys, running with great distinction for Great Britain in the 400m hurdles in the World Championships at Helsinki in August 2005.

J.J.'s philosophy maintains that the key to success lies in the preparation and that winning is the only option. If this win was the result of an exciting display which satisfied the fans, then that was a bonus. To him a 3-0 victory in a dire spectacle was equally rewarding.

J.J. Williams's rugby career began at Maesteg Grammar School where he was chosen to play at outside half. His performances were such that he was soon winning caps for the Welsh Schoolboys. After three years at Cardiff College of Education, he joined Maesteg before moving down the valley to play at the Brewery Field where between 1970 and 1973 he scored 99 tries for his new club in just under a hundred appearances.

But for the short-sightedness of the Welsh selectors of the day, J.J. would have played out his rugby career at Bridgend. For some reasons best known to themselves, they decided against selecting a player from the Bridgend club to play in any of the trial matches preceding the internationals. It was during a match between Llanelli and Bridgend played at Stradey Park that the Llynfi Valley flyer came to a decision which saw him propelled into the rugby spotlight – he decided to join 'the Manchester United of rugby' (his words, not mine!).

While he himself is the first to admit that the transfer was completed purely for selfish reasons (his aim afer all was to play for Wales), J.J. also admired the method of play adopted at Llanelli and was keen to be part of the set-up at Stradey. A meeting was arranged at the home of coach Carwyn James and within days J.J. Williams was officially declared a Llanelli team member. 'From the day I joined the club to the day I retired in 1980, I felt immensely proud each time I pulled on the scarlet jersey. I was determined to repay the faith they had in me.'

J.J. maintains that Llanelli was a 'professional' team thirty years before the concept was formally adopted. In Carwyn James they had a genius as a coach, one who created an efficient, pioneering team around him. This did not just consist of the players on the field, but also involved the committee, along with Norman Gale and Tom Hudson, the latter being responsible for the players' fitness, a concept unheard of at the time. The development of the individual was high on a list of priorities, everyone felt part of the team. They knew the role they had to play and were wholly committed to the cause.

Carwyn's philosophy on the rugby field was to play an expansive game – to get the ball to the backs as quickly as possible so they could get on with the

J.J. in his Lions jersey in 1974.

business of scoring tries. Such a policy was music to the ears of someone with J.J.'s pace. During the weekly training sessions, the coach's voice could be heard time and again as he issued instructions: 'Width, width, width!' Little surprise therefore that this style of rugby attracted the crowds. Indeed in those halcyon days, it was not unusual to see a full house at Abertillery on a cold Wednesday night in February, such was the attraction of the team.

Electrifying speed, a touch of the wizard, a helping of breathtaking audacity – some of the strengths of the wing three-quarter who created such high drama at Stradey Park and beyond in the rugby-playing world. His contribution to the successful Lions tour of South Africa in 1974 is legendary – four tries in four test matches. J.J. also scored tries against England, Scotland, France, Ireland, Australia, South Africa and New Zealand – a remarkable record. He played in 205 matches for Llanelli and scored 159 tries; his international tally is also impressive – 37 appearances (30 Welsh caps and 7 Lions selections) in which he notched up 17 tries.

J.J.'s blistering runs along the touchline were a joy to behold. He never seemed to die with the ball in hand – always managing to pass to one side or the other without breaking his stride. It was J.J. who perfected the art of kicking the ball over his opponent's head, sprinting to retrieve it before pouncing like a leopard catching its prey to touch down for a try. His audacity resulted in 'spectators leaping out of their seats in acclamation'. There have been many moments when the heart has skipped a beat, but none matched the sight of J.J. accelerating and excelling in the scarlet jersey of Llanelli, and the red jerseys of Wales and the Lions.

J.J. (left) reaches for the champagne, as Phil Bennett, Tom David and Carwyn James celebrate another Welsh Cup victory.

31
The Snelling Sevens

i. 'The Magnificent Seven'

Summers always followed a predictable pattern during my teenage years. Weather permitting, Alun Tudur, Elis Wyn, Bleddyn and I would be found at St Helen's in Swansea enjoying the cricket. We would meet up outside Danny, the local butcher's, at 9.30am and be aboard the red double-decker South Wales Transport bus some ten minutes later. Once we had arrived in Swansea, the walk to the cricket ground took us past the YMCA and the old Swansea General Hospital to our theatre of dreams.

Here we would watch in awe as Don and Jim weaved their magic. Here was where Parkhouse and Hedges delivered their batting masterclasses and where some of the best fielders in the world plied their craft – Alan Rees, Allan Watkins, Willie Jones, Jim Pressdee, Billy Slade and the master of them all, Peter Walker.

If the monthly pilgrimage to the cricket had become something of a ritual, soon the annual visit to the Snelling Sevens would follow suit. The venue for the competition alternated between St Helen's, Rodney Parade and Cardiff Arms Park. The crowds would flock in their thousands to enjoy an action-packed display of rugby football. Along the routes to the ground, supporters could be seen laden down with enough sandwiches (usually spam) to feed a battalion, gallons of Vimto, Kia Ora and Tizer, hundreds of Kunzle cakes, and enough sweets to keep dentists busy for months to come.

The first game kicked off at around eleven o'clock in the morning with the final taking place at 6.30pm after which a magnificent Challenge Cup was presented to the winning team, and from 1967 onwards another coveted prize, the Bill Everson Memorial Trophy, was awarded to the best player of the tournament. But what was the magnet that drew the crowds? For those younger readers not familiar with the concept, I will try to explain.

The seven-a-side tournament took place in late spring at the end of the rugby season, overlapping with the start of the cricket, but never compromising the allegiance of its fans. They came in their thousands to enjoy a gala of rugby. The game utilized the whole of the field, but the reduction in the number of players provided an opportunity for those taking part to show off their talents. The stars of the day were all keen to participate, especially the backs, who could go through their repertoire of dummies and sidesteps and swerves.

Reducing the number of players on the pitch has long been adopted in Europe for the development of football players. For several years the Dutch clubs Ajax and Feyenoord have nurtured their youngsters by staging three, four or five-a-side competitions. The credo is that this is a natural way to start learning those basics that they will perfect at a later stage.

The rugby-playing countries of the Southern Hemisphere (and latterly the Rugby Football Union) have also realised the value of such tournaments. Any youngster who exhibits a degree of talent is immediately introduced into the system and then quietly brought along until he realises his full potential.

My first experience of the Snelling Sevens took place in the 1950s when Newport were the undisputed kings. The team, comprising such stalwarts as Ken Jones, Brian Price, Bill Prosser, Brian Jones, David Watkins, Glyn Davidge and Byron Thomas, were unbeatable, and more often than not annihilated the opposition. However, the dawn of a new decade saw a swing in the pendulum and the dominance once enjoyed in the east shifted westward as Llanelli swept all before them. Wyn Oliver, Brian Davies, D. Ken Jones, Onllwyn Brace, Mel Rees, Aubrey Gale and Marlston Morgan were a formidable unit. As a result of their success on the field, the Llanelli committee put in a bid to stage the Snelling Tournament at Stradey Park. Unfortunately, Swansea and the Gwent clubs refused to endorse the proposition (little wonder that the Jacks and the Turks are such arch-rivals to this day!) and the competition was again staged at Cardiff. Revenge was sweet for the Scarlets however, when they brought the cup back across the Loughor Bridge in that same year.

The manner in which the team had played and triumphed was a feast for their supporters. They were ably led by the charismatic Onllwyn Brace, whose ball-handling skills, cunning and trickery often resulted in D. Ken Jones and Brian Davies outmanoeuvring the opposition. This enabled Wyn Oliver to score some spectacular tries which brought the crowd to its feet time and time

Marlston Morgan, the reliable forward showing his skill.

again. However, Bernard 'Slogger' Templeman of Penarth was the hero of the hour. Every time he took possession, an air of excitement and expectation swept around the ground. You just knew something was about to happen, and it usually did! To see 'Slogger' convert was something else – not for him the careful placing of the ball, the hesitant glance at the posts and then the measured run-up. He would just place the ball at his feet and then, with a swing of his right leg and a loud thud, the ball would sail through the air, usually between the uprights!

As we made our way down Queen Street at the end of a very rewarding and satisfactory day and with all of us in festive mood, my attention was drawn to two posters. The headline on both was the same – 'The Magificent Seven'. One, above the Capitol Cinema, referred to Yul Brunner and his motley crowd of gunslingers, but it was the *South Wales Echo* which accurately reflected our feelings. For us, those Llanelli hotshots on that field in Cardiff had been 'The Magnificent Seven'.

Results:

Newbridge	11-6	Aberavon	11-10
Abertillery	8-5	Penarth	14-10

ii. John Bach

Over the years, several 'Johns' have appeared on Llanelli team-sheets – the muscular front-row forward John Warlow (who won his only cap for Wales in Dublin in 1962); the wing forward John Leleu (who later went on to captain Swansea and London Welsh); the left winger John (J.J.) Williams (who became a legend in Llanelli, Wales and Lions jerseys) to name but a few. Added to this list is another John, one who did not achieve the widespread recognition enjoyed by those others, but who nevertheless played no small part in the success Llanelli enjoyed in the late 60s and early 70s. I refer to John 'Bach' Thomas who hailed from the village of Glanaman in the Amman Valley.

As his nickname implies, John Thomas was short of stature, but this in no way detracted from his considerable ball-playing skills. Although he was adept at most sports, football was his first love. The magnificent lawns encompassing the family home afforded John every opportunity of perfecting his skills with the ball. In fact, many of his peers hoped that Wimbledon beckoned as

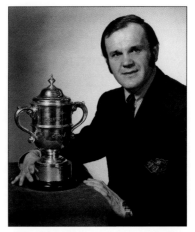

John 'Bach' Thomas, winner of the Bill Everson Trophy, Snelling Sevens 1971.

the neighbouring hospital's tennis courts were within a Roger Federer volley from John's back-door.

During the time that John played in the midfield for Glanaman, he was joined by two other local youngsters who would go on to make their names on the international scene. One was the Wales goalkeeper Dai Davies and the other the late Vernon Pugh, who was to become the Chairman of the International Rugby Board. From the village side, John graduated to play for Ammanford Town, at that time coached by Roy Saunders whose son Dean would later distinguish himself at club and international level. John's impact was such that the local newspaper declared that it would be just a matter of time before the scouts from the big clubs came calling.

This surely would have been the case but for one incident which occurred at the end of the 1967/68 season. Amman United RFC entered a team in the annual Cromwell Evans seven-a-side competition which was being staged at Llandybie. The team set off on their journey with one member of the side absent. The bus had left the Half Moon Hotel and was heading towards the square in Glanaman when John was spotted walking along the street. Already familiar with his talents with a ball, the team captain had no hesitation in stopping the bus and ambushing the startled John at the roadside. After a great deal of coaxing, pleading and cajoling, John Bach was eventually persuaded to join the team and moments later was on his way to Llandybie.

In true fairy-tale fashion, Amman United won the competition with John Thomas playing a pivotal role in the proceedings, controlling play and running elusively. This victory was no small feat for Amman United, for as well as having a new boy in their team, they had also been in competition with Ammanford, Cwmgors, Brynaman, Llandybie and Cwmllynfell who had all fielded strong sides. The end of that season saw him changing codes and opting to play rugby. He excelled in this new code and his team enjoyed a successful run of games, both in fifteen and seven-a-side championships. The latter was particularly eventful as a win in the regional heats at Ammanford propelled Amman United into the National Finals at Aberavon.

Contrary to expectations, the team again reached the final in this competition, narrowly losing by 11-10 to Cardiff College of Education. The Amman United captain, Hywel Evans (now better known as Dafydd Hywel, the renowned actor) led his team to victory over Ebbw Vale, Bridgend and Neath in the preliminary rounds. This was certainly a case of David against several Goliaths! John's performances in each of these games had been nothing short of spectacular. However, it was John's twin brother, David, who had the last laugh. He was a member of the winning Cardiff College of Education team.

After his performances at Aberavon, the scouts did indeed come calling, but they were from Llanelli RFC not from Liverpool, Everton or Arsenal. Three months later John was donning the scarlet jersey of Llanelli and playing at the Stoop in London. Here Llanelli added more silverware to their collection by beating Loughborough Colleges by 19 points to 11 in the final of the tournament. John's contribution to the tally was to score two tries while Keith Hughes, Alan Richards and Selwyn Williams contributed a try apiece.

His first appearance at Stradey Park came on September 1, 1969 when Llanelli played host to La Rochelle. Subsequently John Thomas played regularly for the Scarlets for the next four seasons, establishing himself as a reliable member of the squad and becoming a firm favourite with his fellow players and supporters alike. He may have been short in stature, but he was a formidable opponent. Some described him as a 'corgi' about the field always snapping at his

Hywel Thomas.

opponents' heels and with an innate ability to bring down the biggest adversary. He developed the knack of tackling players around the ankles and embracing them with a vice-like grip so that they were completely immobilised. When Jonah Lomu burst on the international scene in the 1995 World Cup, I was of the opinion that John 'Bach' Thomas would have been the man to mark him.

John himself maintained that Omri Jones of Aberavon and Bob Lloyd of Harlequins had been his most tricky opponents. 'When they ran they used to bring their knees up so high; tackling was difficult.' These defensive qualities were only part of John's repertoire. He also excelled with ball in hand. Aided by that turn of speed, he could quickly spot a gap, and once the advantage was gained he would release a fellow player who was free to create havoc.

John's finest hour came in the 1971 Snelling Sevens tournament played at the National Stadium. Newport had dominated the competition with nine victories since the tournament's inception in 1954 but Llanelli were determined to reverse the trend. In front of 35,000 ecstatic fans, the Scarlets trounced the Black and Ambers 31-10 in the final. The team, comprising Andy Hill, Roy Bergiers, Phil Bennett, John Thomas, Roy Mathias, Arwyn Reynolds and Hefin Jenkins, had been expertly prepared by the doyen of sevens rugby coaches, Hywel Thomas. Now all the hard work bore fruit. To crown an already unforgettable day, John Thomas was awarded the Bill Everson Trophy as the star of the day. He could only reflect on the rugby giants who had preceded him in winning this honour: 1967 David Watkins, 1969 Barry John and now 1971 John Thomas.

Fast forward to 2004, and to a French restaurant *Chez Philippe* in Bordeaux on a night when Llanelli had just lost to Agen. The four of us seated around the dinner table (Phil Bennett, Gareth Charles, Clive Rowlands and myself) were reflecting on some great sevens players of the past. I offered up the name John 'Bach' Thomas. Phil's reply was immediate. 'What a player!' There can be no higher praise.

32

Welsh Rugby Union
Challenge Cup Final 1974

Aberavon 10   Andy Hill 12

The headline may seem a little unfair. There were, after all, fifteen players involved in Llanelli's victory over Aberavon in the final of the WRU Challenge Cup in 1974. Even more remarkably, even though he scored all the points, Andy Hill had been concussed early on in the game. He and the Aberavon centre, Alan Rees, ran for a high ball and the ensuing clash of heads left both players on the ground.

Minutes later, Hill was stepping forward to take a crucial penalty kick. A slight shake of the head was the only indication that things weren't as they should be. Later, Andy was to admit that as he lined up the ball, he realised that he could see four uprights – he was suffering from double vision. Although he had succeeded earlier with two penalty goals, this was proving to be a close match. Time was running out and the pressure to add to the total was mounting. With an excited crowd of 25,000 looking on, Andy Hill

Celebrations off the field – Hefin Jenkins and Andy Hill.

prepared to take one of the most important kicks of his career. That he succeeded in planting the ball between the uprights despite his impaired vision may have been more a matter of luck than judgement, but at any rate those valuable points were acquired. Another penalty goal, minutes before the final whistle, sealed a victory by a hair's breadth.

The result was all the more satisfactory for the Scarlets as they had started the match as underdogs. In a previous encounter held at Stradey Park three weeks earlier, Aberavon had been comfortable winners. This, together with the fact that they had a seriously depleted team – Phil Bennett, Roy Bergiers, J.J. Williams and Tom David were in the Lions squad to tour South Africa – meant that the Llanelli players were not hugely confident as they ran out onto the lush green turf at the National Stadium.

Three minutes into the game saw the first Aberavon score. An attacking break from the Wizards' centre Malcolm Swain resulted in a ruck from which Clive Shell threatened on the blind side. A supporting run from John Bevan ended in a perfectly timed pass to Steve Roper who crossed for a well-worked try. If Allan Martin's conversion kick had not rebounded off the upright, the scores would have been level and Aberavon, as the only try scorers, would have won the match.

Statistics can be used in many ways, sometimes to illustrate a point, or, as is often the case with many politicians, to cloud the truth. In the case of Andy Hill's rugby career the former is undoubtedly true. In a total of 454 games he scored 2577 points which included 310 tries. He was a very reliable wing three-quarter, had a safe pair of hands, never died with the ball and in addition was extremely popular with his fellow players and supporters alike.

Hill's last game for Llanelli was played in 1979, and as he walked off the pitch at Stradey for the last time, Andy was asked whether he felt some disappointment at not having played for Wales despite such a successful career with the Scarlets. His reply speaks volumes about the man's character. 'Yes, I am a little sad, but playing here for twelve seasons in a team that produced such breathtaking rugby has been much more fulfilling than winning one cap whilst representing another team.'

33

These also played at Stradey Park

GEORGE NEPIA (New Zealand)

My grandmother was never a rugby fan. Indeed, she confessed to attending just one match in all of her 82 years. She was amongst the 20,000 spectators present at Stradey Park on December 2, 1924 for the visit of the New Zealand All Blacks. And she was there to support her brother, Jac Elwyn, who was the Llanelli wing three-quarter on that historic day.

The journey from Brynaman to Llanelli was not an easy one in 1924. Leaving her home in Glyn Road, my grandmother would face a brisk walk passing Siloam Chapel and the Farmers' Arms where George Borrow stayed a night on his journey around Wales in the nineteenth century. The G.W.R. steam train would have taken her to Llanelli where there was another long walk to

Stradey Park. Maybe it was the thought of such a trek which deterred her from supporting the game. It would be interesting to know whether now in the 21st century she would have been more interested in watching her great-grandson Shane Williams (Neath, Ospreys, Wales, British Lions) weave his magic on the rugby pitch.

Be that as it may, Maggie Williams could not recall much of the match – not even the score. But she was completely mesmerised by the New Zealand fullback, George Nepia. Her initial reaction had been, 'He shouldn't have been allowed to play. He was so much bigger and stronger than the Llanelli boys!'

The All Blacks won every one of their 30 games during that tour of 1924/25, and George Nepia played a part in each victory. There were some outstanding players in that squad, individuals of the calibre of Cooke, Nicholls, and Brownlie; but it was the nineteen-year-old Nepia, the Blanco, J.P.R. and Christian Cullen, all rolled into one, of his day, who was the undisputed star. As the respected rugby correspondent, Denzil Batchelor wrote, 'It is not for me a question of whether Nepia was the best fullback in history. It is a question of which of the others is fit to loose the laces of his Cotton Oxford boots.'

The New Zealand team also visited South Africa during this period, but without their star player. The apartheid policy in that country at the time meant that the Maoris were not welcome. In 1963 Terry McLean wrote a hugely entertaining biography, entitled *I, George Nepia*. A further tribute was paid to him in 1986, just weeks before his death, in a *This Is Your Life* programme befitting one of the legends of world rugby, one who played at Stradey Park!

HUGO PORTA (Argentina)

29 years ago I knew that I was in the presence of sporting greatness when I saw Hugo Porta step on to the Stradey turf.

I had experienced this same feeling in 1978 at the Wimbledon Tennis Championships. The player in question was the Australian Evonne Goolagong. She oozed talent; a talent which you felt was lurking just under the surface, was kept in tight control but which was liable to explode into devastating life at any moment. It was a feeling repeated in Port of Spain, Trinidad in 1994, during the third test match between the West Indies and England. When Brian Lara strode confidently out to the wicket to face the England bowlers, a buzz of excitement and expectancy filled the ground.

There aren't many sportsmen who can create such an atmosphere before the curtain is raised, but fly half Hugo Porta (and latterly Mark Ring and Shane Williams) can certainly claim this distinction. Following his performance in a midweek match played between Argentina and Wales 'A', Carwyn James wrote in the *Guardian* newspaper, 'For a critic or coach or ex-fly half, it was a question of having one's faith restored in the aesthetic and artistic possibilities of backplay . . .' Thanks to J.K. Rowling, wizards are more or less accepted as a fact of life. Those who saw Porta play that night have long since known it.

The *Sunday Telegraph* correspondent John Reason described Porta as the 'sleepy eyed Clint Eastwood waiting to erupt from under his sombrero'. The French rugby-weekly *Midi Olympique* said of him: *'Porta est un symbole, un chef, le maestro du carousel, l'homme aux pieds d'or, le bon génie de la Pampa, celui qui a donné au rugby Sud-Américain ses lettres de noblesse . . . il donne une merveilleuse sensation d'équilibre et de sérénité ce que représente, à ses yeux, cette "vuelta" dans l'hexagone.'* For those not fluent in French, the translation reads 'bloody fantastic'.

Hugo Porta was until recently Argentina's Sports Minister. Some years ago, I interviewed him in his office in Buenos Aires and found him a modest man, only too willing to share his memories of his rugby-playing days. After some time, the interview came to an end, and with apologies he excused himself. However, he insisted we stay to take refreshments with his secretary.

Over a cup of the best coffee I have ever tasted, the attractive young lady explained that Mr Porta, at 48 years of age, was on his way to play in his weekly football match. She even added proudly that had he chosen to play football instead of rugby, Hugo Porta would have been a member of the Argentina XI which won the World Cup in 1978. And he also played at Stradey!

34

Llanelli 10 New Zealand 16

21 October 1980: A result of political significance

Just because the English close their eyes, it doesn't mean we should forget that the rules exist.

(Urs Meier, one of Switzerland's most experienced referees, who disallowed a late
Sol Campbell goal in the match between England and Portugal at Euro 2004).

One has to accept that in every sphere of life there exist rules which have to be obeyed. There is a certain code of conduct to which we must all adhere. This is especially true in the sporting arena and the person charged with maintaining law and order is the hapless referee. Any decision that he makes is always called into question by one side or the other, meriting column inches in the press and hours of debate in the media and amongst supporters. This is invariably followed up by some (usually good-natured) verbal abuse the next time he returns to the scene of the 'crime'. If an elephant is complimented on his retentive memory, a rugby fan is a close second!

I remember an amusing cricketing story involving a team from the North of England. The occasion was the final of a cup competition, the rivalry between the two teams was intense and there was huge pressure on the incumbent batsman to score runs. The young man taking strike had already swung at and missed several balls. The last ball of the over saw him again attempt a lofted drive and miss, resulting in the wicketkeeper making a loud appeal for a catch. After a suitable interval, the umpire upheld the appeal and raised his finger, and the batsman was on his way back to the pavilion. As he walked past the umpire, he made it plain that he was very unhappy with the decision because his bat had not made contact – in fact he'd missed the ball by about six inches. The umpire, unmoved, declared, 'Look in the *Leader* on Wednesday morning – you'll see from the scorecard that I was right.' The batsman's reply was immediate. 'No, you look,' he said to the umpire 'I'm the Sports Editor!'

During the spring of 1984, I was fortunate enough to spend a month in New England. My brief was to assist in a development programme for referees in that part of the United States. My trip took me from Boston to Vermont, Connecticut, Rhode Island and back to Massachusetts. At each venue I was made to feel welcome and was able to share in the enthusiasm felt for the sport. If sporting authorities in the United States and Canada were to provide facilities and finances for rugby development, then both countries would most definitely become major forces in the game. The fact that players of the calibre of Dave Hodges and Craig Gillies have contributed so much to the Stradey set-up is testament to this fact.

Be that as it may, I found myself one evening in the town of Burlington in the northernmost part of Vermont, some twenty miles from the St Lawrence River and some 40 miles from Montreal. I was to hold a workshop, show some slides and take questions from the enthusiastic gathering. The session went reasonably well, and the evening came to an end with the customary hospitality of a buffet and informal socialising. As I was about to tuck into my Caesar salad and salmon vol-au-vents, I was accosted by a gentleman of generous proportions – he could have been the twin brother of Hoss, the character in the TV series *Bonanza*. Making polite conversation, I enquired how long he had been refereeing and where he had officiated the previous Saturday.

'My last game was last Saturday,' he replied, 'and it was here at Burlington. Mad River played the Lake Champlain Marauders and Mad River won by two points to nil!' It was at this point that my vol-au-vent landed face down on the floor! 'Two points to nil – that's impossible!' was my rather incredulous reply. 'I know that now,' was the fledgling referee's retort, 'but it was a close match, and in the final minutes Mad River managed a push-over try from a scrum followed by a successful conversion. The Marauders were most unhappy with my decision because they were adamant that Mad River had handled whilst the ball was still in the bowels of the scrummage. Whilst sipping a pint in the bar afterwards I realised they were right and I had made a mistake. However, the conversion was perfectly legitimate and went straight through the uprights!'

While the American referee's remarks were utter nonsense, he had at least the good grace to admit to his mistake – a mistake which paled into insignificance when compared with that which took place at Stradey Park on October 21, 1980. For the sixth time in their history, a team from New Zealand made the pilgrimage across the Loughor Bridge to face the might of West Wales rugby. The referee was a member of the Scottish International Panel, the highly respected Alan Hosie. The stage was set for an exciting confrontation with a capacity crowd full of expectation.

The game, as a whole, was an enjoyable one marred occasionally when over-enthusiastic individuals incurred the wrath of the spectators, but not, it seemed, Mr Hosie. I'm sure that as he reflects on his refereeing career, he will agree that this was not one of his better performances. Had he dispatched a few players to the dressing room for an early shower, then he would have gained tighter control of the play. As it was, his failure to do so resulted in a degree of anarchy – players started taking the law into their own hands, and those who should have known better engaged in some ugly off-the-ball activities.

With five minutes of the match remaining, a loud blast emanated from the referee's whistle. Graeme Higginson, the New Zealand second-row forward, was seen to be stamping dangerously on one of the Llanelli forwards who was lying prostrate on the ground. At last, Mr Hosie was going to send a player off, something he himself later admitted he should have done earlier in the match.

A most bizarre incident followed. Ray Gravell, the Llanelli captain and Phil Bennett, the outside half, raced forward and started pleading with the official. Incredibly, they were trying to persuade him not to send the offending player off! A hush descended over the ground as the All Black captain, Graham Mourie, Higginson, players, spectators and commentators alike awaited Mr Hosie's decision. He remarkably blew his whistle and brought the game to an end, with some five minutes left on the clock.

An official statement later maintained that there had been no intention of sending the All Blacks' forward off the field. He had been given a warning. However, it was patently obvious to all those who witnessed the event that but for Ray and Phil's intervention, Higginson would already be in the bath. It is interesting to note that at this point of the game, New Zealand were leading Llanelli by 16 points to 10. A converted try by the home team would have resulted in a draw – a distinct possibility when the opposition were reduced to fourteen men. Now if the American referee from Burlington had been in charge . . .

RAY AND PHIL'S EXPLANATION

Phil Bennett and Ray Gravell – the two peacemakers!

Everyone has an opinion on what went on at Stradey Park that autumn afternoon. This is true in all realms of sport where purists spend hours recollecting, romanticising and re-inventing the past. But despite all the allegations levelled against them, Ray and Phil were only too happy to put the record straight and relive the last moments of that game against the All Blacks. Despite the official statement from Mr Hosie, it does seem that Graeme

Higginson was being dismissed from the field. In such a situation, the captain of the offending player's team is usually the one who pleads with the referee for a degree of leniency on his behalf. But not in this instance. To see Phil and Ray remonstrating with Mr Hosie in such a fashion was bizarre in the extreme. Little wonder that everyone present was thrown into a state of confusion.

Why did they embark on such a course of action? Relations had become strained between Wales and New Zealand during the 1970s and Llanelli were keen to make amends and re-establish a working relationship with their All Black counterparts. To add to the on-field drama, a few other incidents caused concern.

In 1972 Keith Murdoch, the New Zealand prop forward, had been sent home following complaints about his behaviour at the Angel Hotel in Cardiff. Another incident occurred during the famous Barbarians match at the National Stadium when an unpleasant bout of fisticuffs between Grant Batty and Tom David soured proceedings. Yet another infamous incident was to take place in Cardiff in the 1978 test match against Wales. It was alleged that Andy Haden had 'dived' from a line-out. Whether he did or not is open to question, but Mr Quittenton, the referee, was convinced and awarded a penalty to the vistors. Brian McKecknie kicked the goal and Wales lost 13-12.

Given all these facts, the players and officials at Llanelli RFC made a collective decision to try to re-establish good relations with their visitors from the Southern Hemisphere. Yes, this was an important match, and yes, they wanted to win, but as Ray Gravell pointed out, 'The two countries have so much in common – the people, the wonderful landscapes and our love of rugby. It was our responsibility at Stradey to undo all the bad feeling that had begun in the early Seventies and to turn over a new leaf.'

After hearing these words from the Llanelli captain, who could argue with the decision. I'm just grateful the referee was Mr Hosie and not the gentleman from Burlington, Vermont!

35

Swansea vs Llanelli 1983

A fitting tribute

The weekend of January 8, 1983, saw a hastily-arranged meeting between representatives of Llanelli and Swansea rugby football clubs. The former Scarlets' club coach, Carwyn James, had died suddenly whilst on a visit abroad and the subject of the discussions was whether or not the scheduled game between the two clubs, just days after Carwyn's death, should be postponed as a mark of respect.

After some deliberation, it was decided that the match would proceed as planned. For their part, the Llanelli delegation agreed that the highest tribute the club could offer would be a victory secured with the flair and panache that Carwyn had come to expect of the team. At that point in the season, there was little to separate the two teams in the league table but Swansea had won their last seventeen matches and were clear favourites to beat Llanelli at St Helen's.

An inspirational pre-match team talk from Ray Gravell proved one of many catalysts that day. A minute's silence was observed, after which the whole of St Helen's exploded into a cacophony of sound. Emotions were riding high on both sides, with even a few Whites' supporters (albeit grudgingly) hoping that the Scarlets would win.

Although Mark Wyatt's penalty goal gave Swansea an early lead, as the game progressed, the Scarlets started to gain the upper hand. A long kick downfield by their outside half, Geraint John, resulted in a Scarlets throw-in at the line-out from which Phil May forced his way over the try-line. Kevin Thomas's conversion ensured that the interval scoreboard read: Swansea 3 Llanelli 6.

With the elements favouring them in the second half, the All Whites kicked off with a renewed air of purpose and confidence. But they had reckoned without the almost fanatical desire of the Llanelli XV to do Carwyn proud and soon a second try followed for the Scarlets. Peter Hopkins broke through a tackle, released Kevin Thomas who then put David Nicholas in at the corner flag. Geraint John played like a man possessed and it was his probing that allowed Peter Hopkins to score his team's third try.

Another player who proved to be a real thorn in the Swansea side was wing forward, David Pickering. No sooner had he put in one tackle than he would pop up half a pitch away in equally destructive mode. An unforgiving duel also took place between the respective scrum halves, as the Douglas brothers – Mark (for the Scarlets) and Carl (Swansea) – faced one another for the first time at this level.

When the final whistle blew Llanelli were victors by 16 points to 9. And as the *South Wales Evening Post* columnist wrote the following evening, 'Carwyn James would have approved. They didn't just take Swansea apart – they did it in style!'

Geraint John – the outside half turned coach.

36
'I'm from The Guardian'

I'm not sure whether Mr Murdoch would be interested in incorporating it into his media empire, but there exists in the Amman Valley a newspaper which has straddled several decades and generations. The *South Wales Guardian* is a local newspaper which records in the minutest detail the exploits of those villages within its circulation. These exploits may include success in the sporting arena and the academic world, or records of births, deaths and marriages, and the like.

One of the newspaper's reporters lived in our street and I vividly remember his timetable during the winter months. Each Saturday his afternoon would begin at Cwmllynfell where he would take notes for some ten minutes before climbing into his A30 for the short journey to the rugby field at Brynaman. At half-time he would continue in his role as roving reporter and move on to Cwmgors, Garnant and finally end up in Ammanford for the last few minutes of the match there.

Four days later, when the weekly publication dropped through the letter box, accounts of each match played would appear under the pseudonym *Hawkeye*. The aim of the author and the newspaper in general was to highlight the achievements of the local clubs and hopefully gain some recognition for any promising young players in their midst.

I have referred in another chapter to the fact that during the 1970s I was an avid reader of *The* (Manchester) *Guardian* newspaper. Among their excellent coterie of correspondents were the sports writers Frank Keating and of course Carwyn James. Not only were these two professional colleagues but they were also to become close friends. In fact, Frank Keating could be considered a true friend of Welsh rugby as he often sang its praises in his intelligently-written, honest and often witty columns.

In 1983 he published a rugby 'diary' entitled *Up and Under*. This has proved to be a classic among sporting books. So popular was the publication that it became a bestseller and proved to all who read it that rugby was a game to be loved and to be enjoyed.

Towards the end of the book, Frank Keating gives an account of his journey to Cefneithin to attend the funeral of his colleague Carwyn James. The road from Cross Hands and Gorslas to Tabernacl Chapel, where the service was to be held, was choked with cars. It seemed that the whole of Wales and beyond wanted to pay their last respects to the great man. The chapel was full to the rafters with hundreds of mourners standing outside, hoping to catch a little of the service that was taking place within.

Desperate to be a part of the proceedings, Keating approached an usher who was guarding one of the doors, and explained his predicament. 'Please, can't you squeeze me in? I'm from *The Guardian*.' Bowing respectfully, the gentleman replied that he would do his best. The two men made their way towards the front of the chapel only to be greeted by a sea of faces and not one empty seat. As he was about to escort the journalist back to the door, the usher spotted a space right underneath the pulpit and between the BBC equipment being used to transmit the funeral service.

'Move over please.' he said to one mourner. 'This gentleman is from the *South Wales Guardian*.' That would have brought a wry smile to Carwyn's face.

Frank Keating – 'from *The Guardian*'!

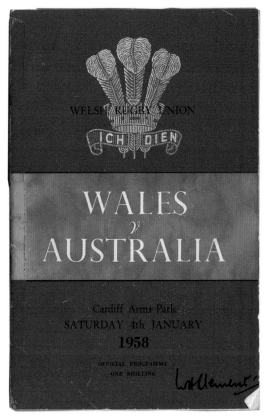

The match programme of Carwyn's first cap.

118

37

The Schweppes Cup Final 1985

A momentous day for Gary Pearce and Phil May

During the Seventies and Eighties, the yardstick by which any rugby team in Wales was measured was their success in the Schweppes Cup. Llanelli's record in this competition during the initial decade was second to none. They appeared in five consecutive finals and lost just one, beating Cardiff in 1973, Aberavon in 1974 and 1975 and Swansea in 1976. The showcase final was held in early May at the National Stadium in Cardiff where fans flocked in their thousands to enjoy the carnival atmosphere.

The years that followed the 1976 season, however, saw a change in fortune in the club's success. There were changes in personnel and many of those experienced players who had formerly served the club so well, were now in the twilight of their career and could no longer maintain the high standards required. These were just a few of the reasons put forward to explain the decline. While it is true that there was the occasional glimpse of the glory days of the past with a victory over a visiting overseas side, these were few and far between.

The powers that be at Llanelli soon came to realise that they were no longer at the forefront of rugby development in Wales. Clubs such as Cardiff, Pontypool, Newport and Swansea had made great strides whereas Llanelli had remained static. The club that was once considered the best in Britain found itself in something of a crisis.

Following John Maclean's retirement as team coach in 1982, it was decided that two former players in the persons of Gareth Jenkins and Allan Lewis would be appointed to take charge. Allan had honed his coaching skills at Ammanford, Pontarddulais and Penygroes while Gareth had served his coaching apprenticeship at Furnace. These two proved inspirational choices. The duo decided almost immediately to lay waste the ghosts of the late Seventies and early Eighties and to resurrect Carwyn James's mantra – to play open, expansive, entertaining rugby. Success followed very quickly with a surprise win against the 1982 Maoris following in the footsteps of the successful teams of 1888 and 1926. Indeed four of the players from that 1926 side were spectators at Stradey sixty years on – Ivor Jones, Ernie Finch, Rees Thomas and Emrys Griffiths. Unfortunately, this result did not set the pattern for the rest of the season which proved to be a comparatively modest one for the club. Undaunted, officials and supporters alike agreed that this was a period when team-building and general improvements were the primary objectives. Llanelli did manage to reach the semi-final of the Cup but were heavily defeated by Cardiff by 6-26; an accurate reflection of the chasm which separated the two teams.

The 1984/85 season started with the media, and *The Western Mail* in particular, forecasting a bumper year for the Blue and Blacks. No one would argue that Cardiff had a very strong team – the forwards were powerful, and in Whitefoot, Phillips and Eidman they had the best front row in Britain. Added to this was the towering presence of Robert Norster in the second row, widely considered one of the best line-out jumpers in the world. It is easy to see why the halfbacks Terry Holmes and Gareth Davies had free rein to dictate the course of each match.

As the season progressed, the Cardiff side lived up to expectations with many notable wins and very few losses marked against them. With the new coaches settling in to the task of rebuilding, Llanelli were beginning to resemble the team that swept all before in the halcyon days of the Seventies. Thus Saturday, April 27, 1985 saw the Scarlets take on Cardiff at the National Stadium in the final of the Schweppes Cup. I'm sure it is true to say that the majority of the 40,000 supporters present, if asked, would have their money on a Cardiff win. Fifteen Llanelli players and two determined coaches thought otherwise.

Cardiff were the bookies' favourite to win the cup and Cardiff should have won the cup. They were however outwitted and outmanoeuvred in a most subtle and frustrating manner! Phil May, the Llanelli skipper, realised very early on in the proceedings that the referee, Derek Bevan, was turning a blind eye to any misdemeanours in the lines-out. The result of this was that the Llanelli forwards had carte blanche to disrupt and create mayhem in this phase of play. Nothing illegal, you understand, just a stray arm here, or an elbow there, but it meant that the Blue and Blacks could not control and deliver quick ball to their dangerous halfbacks.

Throughout the season the Cardiff pack had been totally dominant and had provided endless opportunities for their skilful three-quarters. Ring, Hadley and Cordle had been able to go through a whole repertoire of moves and points had been gathered at regular intervals. However, thanks to the spoiling tactics employed by the Llanelli forwards, the Blue and Blacks could not put together any cohesive moves, the result of which was an evenly-contested match. Unlike many cup finals, which despite the hype beforehand often turn out to be dire affairs, this proved to be a white-knuckle ride for both sets of supporters, with the advantage swinging back and forth like a metronome.

With only a few minutes left to play, Cardiff were ahead by 14 points to 12 and were confident that they could defend this advantage. This is when fate played its hand. The Llanelli forwards won the ball at a line-out and dispatched it to the halfbacks. When Gary Pearce took possession, he was positioned some ten metres in from the touchline and some thirty metres from the posts. As 40,000 pairs of eyes inside the stadium and thousands more at home watched, he took aim and propelled the Gilbert oval high into the air and straight between the uprights. It was, without question, one of the sweetest drop goals kicked in Scarlet colours since Harry Bowen's remarkable effort against the Maoris in 1888.

It seemed that all those hours on the practice fields at Laugharne, Bridgend and Stradey were in preparation for this moment. The crowd went wild with excitement, which was, however, tempered by no little anxiety, as no one was quite sure how much injury time Mr Bevan would add to the allotted forty minutes. Llanelli were ahead by 15 points to 14 with the clock ticking by. A quick consultation between the referee and two captains confirmed that the next time the whistle was blown it would be for no-side. Gareth Davies's restart kick reached the Llanelli ten-metre line. Unforgivably, the Scarlet forwards failed to gather and the ball was gift-wrapped into the welcoming hands of the Cardiff forwards. In an instant, Gareth Davies, the Cardiff fly half, positioned himself for a match-winning drop goal. He was a master of this particular art, and all present prepared to see the ball sailing between the uprights towards the river Taff.

However, thanks to a heroic leap and fingertip save from the Scarlet No. 8, Phil Davies, the ball changed its trajectory and veered off to the left of the posts. The referee blew his whistle and that was it – Llanelli, against all the odds, had won the Cup! This was the beginning of a period of renaissance in the annals of Llanelli Rugby Football Club. There would be no more harping back to the glorious Seventies!

Celebrating Gary Pearce's drop goal: unforgettable moments.

38

The power of two

As demonstrated by the scoreline: Llanelli 13 Australia 9

It is a sad and undeniable state of affairs that when it comes to choosing a 'British' team, Welsh sportsmen and women appear to be a forgotten entity. For those of us brought up on an annual diet of school and national eisteddfodau, the claim that a competitor had been 'robbed' often rang loud and true. Was it not, after all, the subjective opinion of adjudicators that determined the individual's success or failure?

In the realms of sport this should not be the case. Here, there are several yardsticks of individual performance, statistics being the most obvious one. But however impressive these figures appear, they seem to count for nothing when arguing the case for those who live to the west of the Severn Bridge or the Mersey Tunnel. Over several seasons Glamorgan County Cricket Club has, for example, consistently produced top-class players. Alan Jones, Don Shepherd, Matthew Maynard, Steve Watkin, Hugh Morris and Steve James are only a few who spring to mind. These cricketers played in a team that was consistently in the top half of championship tables, but were largely ignored by the test-match selectors. Thankfully, the current set-up selects players on merit.

On the football field, selectorial blunders deprived Dave Bowen's XI of immortality. Who knows if the inclusion of Ray Daniel and Trevor Ford would have resulted in a World Cup win in Sweden in 1958? The men who stride the corridors of power at the Welsh Rugby Union also seem to have a blinkered viewpoint when it comes to making crucial decisions. At the beginning of the 1990s, Gareth Jenkins and Allan Lewis were arguably the best coaches in Wales, if not in Britain. Their role model and mentor was the late, great Carwyn James and it was his philosophy that was then being replayed at Stradey Park.

Although it was widely assumed that Gareth was the chief coach, with Allan playing a supporting role, the duo did not see it that way. Theirs was a partnership in the true sense of the word. Gareth assumed responsibility for the forwards, preparing them both physically and mentally for battle while at the same time working on a strategy which would benefit the team as a whole. He was in charge of the 'juggernauts'. Allan, on the other hand, took charge of the 'ballerinas', the backs. His job was to develop their potential, stimulate creativity and generally fine-tune what had been prepared on the practice field.

The partnership proved a very successful one and produced the style of rugby of which William Webb Ellis would have been proud. But, typically, as the team earned plaudits from far and near, the call from the Taf Mahal to take charge of the national side did not materialise. It is true that there was a token

Gareth Jenkins.

Allan Lewis.

attempt to include them, albeit in a supporting capacity: Gareth became part of Alan Davies's management team, whilst Allan undertook duties on Graham Henry's behalf.

When there were vociferous demands for a complete shake-up at HQ, and an improvement in standards, it was to the Southern Hemisphere that the 'suits' turned for guidance. Clive Rowlands, himself a former inspirational national coach and Lions tour manager, argued against this. He was totally opposed to appointing coaches from overseas. He was adamant that we had the required calibre of personnel in Wales. On reflection, and in light of our Grand Slam win in 2005, I believe that Clive was correct in his assessment.

We can only wonder at what might have been, but there is no question that in tandem, Gareth Jenkins and Allan Lewis were a force to contend with. Theirs was a symbiotic partnership, born of mutual respect, and was the envy of many a team. Since their parting of the ways, Gareth has gone on to steer Llanelli to a Celtic League championship and two Heineken Cup semi-finals, as well as numerous Welsh Cup and Championship successes. Allan has been instrumental in rebuilding teams such as Moseley, Newport (a Welsh Cup win), Bridgend (a deserved Championship victory during season 2002/03) and latterly (until that region was suddenly disbanded in the summer of 2004) the Celtic Warriors.

Whilst at Stradey Park, the pair's finest hour came on December 14, 1992. The visitors were the World Cup holders, Australia. Even the most optimistic of supporters recognized that the task ahead was an awesomely daunting one. The Wallaby side selected for the encounter was a strong one, which was by way of a compliment to Llanelli. It also showed that the Australians were desperate to win.

From the kick-off, it was obvious what the Scarlets' intentions were. They were no respecters of reputations and the tackling from the outset was ferocious. Although Australia kept winning a steady supply of possession, they weren't able to play with the flair and abandon which had enabled them to conquer the rugby world. The Scarlets pack played its socks off with Phil Davies, Mark Perego and Emyr Lewis appearing to be supercharged for the confrontation.

LLANELLI AUSTRALIA

v

Huw Williams	15	Marty C. Roebuck
Ieuan Evans	14	Paul V. Carozza
Nigel Davies	13	Tim P. Kelaher
Simon Davies	12	Jason S. Little
Wayne Proctor	11	Damian Smith
Colin Stephens	10	Tim G. Horan
Rupert Moon (Captain)	9	Peter J. Slattery
Ricky Evans	1	Dan J. Crowley
Andrew Lamerton	2	Phil N. Kearns (Captain)
Laurance Delaney	3	Ewan J. A. McKenzie
Phil Davies	4	Rod J. McCall
Anthony Copsey	5	John A. Eales
Mark Perego	6	David Wilson
Emyr Lewis	8	B. Tim Gavin
Lyn Jones	7	Willie Ofahengaue

Replacements

Gary Jones		Anthony Ekert
Paul Jones		Paul Kahl
David Joseph		Darren Junee
Barry Williams		David V. Nucifora
Steve Wake		Andrew Blades
Neil Boobyer		Troy Coker

Heroes, one and all.
The only replacement to feature was Dai Joseph for Laurance Delaney.
Coaches: Gareth Jenkins and Allan Lewis.

124

Simon Davies, the Llanelli centre, was another, resembling a heat-seeking missile intent on Marty Roebuck's destruction wherever he appeared on the field. On more than one occasion when it seemed as if the Wallaby fullback had broken free, Davies, his menacing shadow, was there to bring him down and thwart any potential move.

Also outstanding (on an afternoon of inspired performances) was Huw Williams at fullback. He was a late replacement for the injured Ian Jones, but took full advantage of his opportunity, producing the performance of a lifetime. One particular incident stood out when in tackling Tim Horan, the Australian outside-half, he literally lifted the Wallaby off his feet before dumping him unceremoniously head first into the mud.

Simon Davies, a creative and destructive centre.

Only one try was scored during the game – but it was a cracker. More than that, it was scored by the Scarlets! It came from a move perfected on the training 'paddock' and once again demonstrated that sparkle which seems part and parcel of Llanelli's folklore. Its catalyst was fly half Colin Stephens. With ball in hand, he feigned on two occasions to release two team-mates and in the process created a huge void for Ieuan Evans to explore. The wing three-quarter, appeared like a genie out of a lamp, received the ball at pace and darted over near the posts. The 15,000 crowd was on its feet, the try resulting in a cheer which could be heard from Cydweli to Cynheidre.

With a minute left to the end of the match, the scoreboard read Australia 9 Llanelli 7. What followed could have been written by Tarantino or Spielberg – it was of such high drama. With the ball in hand Colin Stephens, deaf to the desperate calls from his centres, decided to attempt a drop goal. It was poorly struck and prompted groans from the nervous spectators around the ground. However, as in all the best dramas, there came a twist at the end. For all its questionable trajectory, and as everyone looked on in stunned silence, the ball just went on and on and miraculously scraped its weary way over the bar! It was only when the referee raised his arm in confirmation that everyone realised the significance of the young man's effort.

The cheer that went up to greet the try was nothing compared with the eruption that greeted the announcement of the score: Llanelli 10 Australia 9. With his confidence now stratospheric, the outside half added another drop goal for good measure The final result read Llanelli 13 Australia 9. There were fifteen heroes on display at Stradey Park that afternoon, but we must not forget the two magnificent coaches.

Colin Stephens: a quicksilver fly half.

39

The Front-row Freemasons

i. The prop forwards

Like the special ingredient handed down in an old family recipe, or the combination to the vault in the Bank of England, what goes on in the front row of a scrum is a secret known only to a select few. If one had the time, or the inclination, it might be possible to trawl through the archives of the National Library at Aberystwyth in search of such information, but it would be to no avail. As with any apprenticeship, this particular knowledge is passed on by word of mouth and the lessons of experience, and there aren't many who can be considered as masters of the craft.

Those who have tasted the peculiar delights of playing in the front row of the scrum compare it with a period spent in a medieval dungeon, or of working in cramped conditions on the coalface. It is certainly not for the faint-hearted.

Following a recent defeat at the hands of Biarritz, one of the Stradey faithful was heard to remark, 'Gosh, those Basque props actually look like props! Iestyn and John resemble 100-metre athletes!' The remark cannot be easily refuted. While it is true that modern players need to be athletic, the hours spent in the gymnasium have completely altered the physical demeanour of the front-row forward. They are now to be seen running all over the field, tackling anyone that moves, and even at times forming part of the back line in support of a wing three-quarter! Has all this been at the expense of perfecting their own, more clandestine, technique?

The prop forward is traditionally seen as a man-mountain; a strong, physical, solid individual with a powerful upper body. His primary function is to maintain stability in the scrummage. Nowhere was this concept more obviously demonstrated than by the Biarritz props, Denis Avril and Petru Balan, during the game at Stradey. Over the years, Llanelli has produced many great prop forwards who have gone on to win international honours, and they include Tom Evans, the Revd Alban Davies, Gethin Thomas, Edgar Jones, Harry Truman, Griff Bevan, Henry Morgan, John Warlow, Barry Llewellyn, Anthony Buchanan, Laurance Delaney, Ricky Evans, Huw Williams-Jones, Spencer John, Iestyn Thomas, and Martyn Madden.

John Davies, the tight-head prop, who hails from the West Wales village of Boncath, won 34 caps for his country and should have won many more. Interestingly, these honours were attained whilst John was a member of firstly Neath, and then the Richmond squad. Although he has maintained his excellent high standards at Llanelli, bizarrely the Welsh selectors ignored his presence. Another case of déjà vu. Nevertheless Wales's loss proved to be Llanelli's gain.

John Davies on one of his trademark charges.

John started his first-class career at the Gnoll. Ron Waldron was the Welsh All Blacks' coach at the time, and it was he who was responsible for developing the now legendary front-row trio of Brian Williams, Kevin Phillips and John Davies. These three West Wales farmers proved to be a strong, powerful unit who caused untold problems for rugby teams up and down the land.

During the practice sessions, Waldron would spend hours drilling the forwards in the mechanics of scrummaging. His philosophy of 'back to basics' was in evidence years before the ethos was adopted by the Tory Prime Minister, John Major. While recognising the importance of these first principles, the team's undoubted forte was the ability to launch an attack from any given situation. This was a new concept in Welsh rugby at the time, and involved Brian initially making a break with ball in hand. As soon as he was held, the ball would be released to either Kevin or John who would continue the movement maintaining a frantic momentum. This was contrary to the usual tactic of creating rucks and mauls after the initial tackle. All these movements were accomplished at breakneck speed, and proved to be extremely effective for the Neath side and extremely difficult for a defending team to resist.

What he learned at the Gnoll in those early days has now become an integral part of John Davies's mode of play. It is not unusual to see the prop's Scarlet jersey suddenly emerge from a mound of bodies and thunder towards the try-line clutching the ball safely in his hands. Not for him the listless hovering on the winger's touchline. No, he is in there, in true prop-forward fashion, in the thick of the action.

In this current period, John Davies is a true professional. Even when he has had to attend to the duties of his other calling, that of a farmer, his commitment to the game has never been brought into question. I recall the days he spent playing at the Gnoll. A typical day would begin with his early morning duties at the farm. Once completed, a drive to Cardiff would follow for a training session with the Welsh squad. Late afternoon would find John snatching a short siesta in his parked car outside the Gnoll. Just before seven o'clock he would pull on another set of kit and jog out to train with the Neath team. Once this was over, he would then face the long drive back home to Boncath. If this was not the sign of a truly dedicated professional, then I defy anyone to suggest otherwise.

Laurance Delaney – another name which conjures up the image of a stereo-typical prop forward. Laurance was an outstanding scrummager, and as such he was held in high esteem by his peers, even if they did not enjoy the weekly contretemps in the front row as much as Laurance himself!

He took his responsibilities in the scrum very seriously, and his aim at all times was to make sure that his hooker was well served. To this end he employed a whole range of techniques which varied according to which scrum half was to feed the ball into the scrum. If it was a Llanelli put-in, then Laurance had his feet planted solidly on the ground and used his considerable strength and know-how to maintain equilibrium and provide a clear path for the hooker to get to the ball.

But if the opposing side had the put-in, then different strategies were implemented, not all of which adhered strictly to the law book! Laurance relished this role, that of causing chaos in a defensive scrum. His aim of course was to drag down his opponent so that their hooker was unsighted, and

Laurance on the attack against Aberavon, with Kerry Townley in support.

all without attracting the attention of the referee. He was so adept at this that the movement often went undetected until the damage had been done.

Laurance Delaney played 501 games for Llanelli and won 11 caps for Wales. His spell in the national team coincided with a difficult period in Welsh rugby when it was suffering from a lack of leadership and direction. Who knows how many more caps Laurance would have amassed in another decade or century? In these times of ever-evolving technology, there is still a need for certain practical skills. These may include plumbing, carpentry, roofing, and most certainly tight-head propping!

ii. Hookers

I can accept failure; everyone fails at something. But I can't accept not trying.

Michael Jordan might well have had certain individuals in mind when he made the above observations, but the charge of not trying can never be levelled at the players who have worn the No. 2 jersey for Llanelli RFC. These men are a breed apart – in fact they even appear to possess a different genetic make-up from the rest of us mortals. A glance along a gallery of photographs of incumbents of the position is all it takes to verify this fact. What therefore are the attributes needed to play in this position? What is the role of the hooker and what part does he play in the general scheme of things?

The duties of a hooker have changed dramatically over the last decade. What is expected of Robin McBryde is light years away from the skills employed by Norman Gale in the 1960s. In the latter's case, his main objective was to win the ball in the scrum. This was to be done at any cost, and if the strike was against the head, all the better, for the psychological advantage gained by his team as a result was immense.

Nowadays, the hooker has replaced the wing three-quarter as the player who throws in the ball at a line-out. This change came about in the Seventies which meant that Bryn Evans, Mel Rees and Norman Gale were exempt from the hours of practice now spent in perfecting the technique. It is said that Robin McBryde spent more of his time with his fellow forwards than he did with his own family! Such is the need to perfect the art of accurately finding your man in the line-out.

This change of direction in a hooker's duties does come at a cost. It is a rare sight these days to see a team winning a strike against the head. All the basic elements of binding and driving seem to be in place but nothing more – the hookers of old would have strained every muscle and sinew to get at the ball. The tactics involved were not always legal, but in the cauldron that is the scrum, even the most diligent of referees could not always ensure that fair play prevailed.

Llanelli can boast a long line of extremely competent hookers – Mathew Rees, Robin McBryde, Andrew Lamerton, Kerry Townley, Howard Thomas, Arwyn Reynolds, David Fox, and Norman Gale. Any one of these players could have claimed a place in a top-quality club side. Roy Thomas was another notable member of this unique group, whose talent was not recognised by the national selectors. His permanent position as replacement meant that he could have turned up on match day in his best suit to take his seat on the bench, so confident was he that he would not be called upon to take to the field.

Unfortunately for Roy, he was in competition with the Pontypool hooker, Bobby Windsor. There are those who would argue that the two were on a par, and that Roy was just unlucky. Luck did play a cruel trick on Roy Thomas in 1979. Bobby Windsor was forced to pull out of the game against England as a result of a burn he sustained after falling on some lime at Pontypool Park. A

Derek Quinnell, Charles Thomas and Roy Thomas in the thick of it against Bridgend.

replacement was needed, but as Roy had retired the previous season, Alan Phillips, the Cardiff hooker, was summoned to fill the breach. Roy's only international game was played against Tonga in 1975 – to add insult to injury the team played in green (Tonga wore red jerseys) and no caps were awarded. *C'est la vie!*

Robin McBryde was another ever-present in the middle of the Llanelli front row. After a number of seasons spent playing for Swansea, Robin decided to join the exodus across the Loughor Bridge and became a part of the Stradey set-up. He became a highly respected and inspirational part of the team and won plaudits both nationally and internationally.

Like the prop forward John Davies, Robin's commitment to the Llanelli cause is absolute. He is enthusiastic, dedicated and never shies away from his responsibilities. When he is not charging around the field, he can be seen unexpectedly popping out from a maul, ball in hand, having wrestled it away from his opponent. He is not afraid to take on an adversary, big or small. Off the field, Robin is a modest, self-effacing, extremely likeable individual; a role model for any youngster interested in playing rugby football.

Among many legends who have donned the Scarlet shirt of Llanelli, no one has worn it with more pride than the late Norman Gale. Captain of his country in 1967 and the winner of 25 caps (his first won in Dublin when he replaced

131

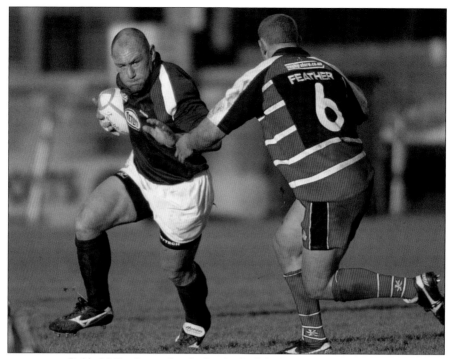
Robin McBryde wearing the Scarlets' original colours (1875-1879).

the injured Bryn Meredith), Norman was a true professional in what was then an amateur game. Born in the village of Gorseinon, Norman Gale was destined to play hooker from the moment he could crawl. He himself would agree that his looks could not compete with the George Clooneys and Brad Pitts of this world, but his attitude and demeanour would certainly be used as a role model for a Bruce Willis or Gene Hackman film. Not only did Norman look and sound threatening – he was both!

He was the type of person you would choose to escort you if you had to venture into the South Side of Chicago or the dockyard area of Marseilles. I'm sure Al Capone would have employed him as one of his henchmen, merely from glancing at his photograph.

Nothing gave Norman more pleasure than to make his presence felt on the rugby field. He was not a dirty player but he certainly relished the physical aspects of the sport. Within the dark depths of the scrum there may not be an outright war but there are certainly battles going on which may not relate directly to the game. Suffice it to say, that whatever the situation, Norman could stand his ground, and more often than not, could come away victorious.

There are two interesting anecdotes which illustrate his physical prowess and commitment. In Durban, South Africa in 1964, and under a blazing sun, Wales suffered their heaviest defeat in forty years. The score at half-time was 3-3 but the physical effort of running around and tackling continuously in such conditions had taken a heavy toll on the Welsh players. According to certain reports, there were just two Welshmen on their feet during the interval sampling the cooling water and Outspans – the No 8. John Mantle and Norman Gale. The rest of the team were, understandably, scattered around the park like rag dolls exhausted by their efforts, before going on eventually to lose by 24-3.

The second incident occurred in a match in Auckland, New Zealand, in 1969. Again Wales were well beaten by 33-12 (Fergie McCormick creating a new world record with a personal tally of 24 points) and the contest, in typical All Black fashion, was a physical one with no quarter asked or given by either side. Leading the charge for Wales – Norman Reginald Gale! The likes of Meads, Gray, McLeod, Smith and Hopkinson held no fears for him!

Norman Gale successfully served Llanelli RFC in many capacities – as player, captain, coach, and chairman. Our paths often crossed during the Seventies and Eighties when I found myself refereeing at Stradey Park. Mind you, most referees in those days kept out of his way! He might have been a man of few words, but if he felt that his team had suffered an injustice – then he was very vocal and made his point strongly. To his credit, everyone agreed that Norman had a thorough understanding of the game which made the criticism a little easier to take.

After retiring from the world of rugby, for many years he became steward of the White Horse, a public house within kicking distance of Stradey Park. A more relaxed Norman Gale presented a softer, warmer side to his personality. He remains one of the legends of Llanelli Rugby Football Club.

The captain leading Wales into battle, 1967.

133

40

Scavengers and tinkers

The back-row boys.

According to the Irish writer Ulrick O'Connor, the tinkers are a class of people who are audacious enough to steal from right under a person's nose: 'Why, even the froth on the top of your Guinness isn't safe!' Their rugby union equivalent, if they are doing their job properly, are back-row forwards. It is their duty to scavenge around the field in search of the ball, before stealing it from right under their opponents' noses. And, very often, under the referee's nose too!

We all have our favourites. Some at Stradey will even admit that there have been some fine opposition back-rowers, Arthur Lemon, Clem Thomas, Haydn Morgan, Alun Pask, Dai Morris, Omri Jones, Chris Huish and Martyn Williams – to name but a few. But the club itself can boast a list of players who have served their tinker apprenticeship at Stradey Park. One such was Archie Skym who hailed from the village of Drefach, near Tumble. He had the singular honour of playing in the front, second and back rows for Wales during the Twenties and Thirties. His strength and his speed around the field were legendary and, coupled with his resilience and stamina, made him a formidable opponent.

Another outstanding player from this era was Watcyn Thomas. He was an inspirational leader and as a line-out jumper he was acknowledged by the New Zealand All Blacks as one of the best ever. Thomas captained Wales when they achieved their first victory at Twickenham in 1933. Two years earlier he had shown great courage in the game against Scotland. Despite suffering a broken collarbone during the early part of the match, he carried on playing for the next sixty minutes and scored a try to boot.

Other notable back-row players from the Thirties were Jim Lang, a member of the national XV who beat the All Blacks at Cardiff in 1935, and Ossie Williams who was never far from the action.

During the Sixties I was a frequent visitor to Stradey Park, and I can remember being completely enthralled with the range of skills exhibited by Clive John, one of the famous John brothers from Cefneithin. According to his brother Barry (and surely he would know), Clive was the most gifted of the three brothers. For those supporters who flocked to watch Llanelli at this time, the artistry displayed by the younger brother at times equalled, if not eclipsed, those of 'The King' himself.

'They seek him here, they seek him there . . .' are words which could have been penned with Clive John in mind. He was like a ghost about the field. An opponent would close in for a tackle, only to realise in the blink of an eye that they were grasping thin air! Clive John started his rugby-playing career with

Clive John on the attack against Newport.

the Llanelli Youth team. During his final season he claimed over 50 tries and was eventually promoted to the senior side partnering brother Barry against Rosslyn Park in 1966. It was a proud moment for the John family who that day saw two of its members turn out in the scarlet strip of Llanelli. Their brother Alan, a tearaway open-side wing forward, was also a Stradey regular for many seasons in the Sixties.

It was as a blind-side wing forward however that Clive gained recognition. He had that innate ability to free himself from the most secure tackle, could weave his way through the opposing forwards with consummate ease, and his running angles created mayhem in opposition defences. His style of play is what the modern-day player aspires to, and his ability to change the tempo of a movement in an instant led to opportunities for others.

Clive was a natural choice because of his versatility to be part of the Lions squad to tour Australia and New Zealand in 1971. Sadly for him, he broke his arm while playing for the Wales 'B' XV against France on the eve of the tour party's announcement. As a result, of course, he missed out on what would have been certain international honours. This injury proved to be the beginning of a whole catalogue of mishaps which were to haunt him over the next few seasons, and which forced him to give up playing rugby football. Although he could no longer play, Clive did take an active role as coach to several West Wales teams – a role in which he enjoyed great success.

Another faithful servant during the seventies was the No. 8, Hefin Jenkins. He was destined for international honours, and would have won many a cap had he not had the misfortune of playing at the same time as the legendary Wales and British Lions No. 8 forward, Mervyn Davies. On the one occasion

Hefin Jenkins challenging the Pontypool scrum half.

when Mervyn was sidelined through injury, fate dealt a cruel blow as Hefin too was incapacitated with an ankle problem.

According to his fellow players, Hefin was not only a talented rugby player, but also an excellent ambassador for the game. Off the field he was a gentleman, but once he donned the scarlet jersey he metamorphosed into a hard, physical presence who constantly caused chaos from the base of the scrum. He was a first-class line-out jumper and his handling skills were such that he proved to be an effective link between forwards and backs.

Since his retirement as a player, Hefin has served the club in an administrative capacity, doing so with the same distinction as he did as a player. And over the last few seasons he has seen many back-row forwards from the Llanelli squad go on to receive international honours: players such as Mark Perego, David Pickering, Lyn Jones, David Hodges and Simon Easterby. The future looks promising with Dafydd Jones, Alix Popham and Gavin Thomas now picking up the mantle.

To be able to play in the back row, a modern-day player needs to be strong, athletic, and have a clear understanding of what is taking place around him. A boundless supply of energy is required and in addition, one also needs the patience of a Job, the determination of a David and the wisdom of a Solomon. To be all of the above requires a certain calibre of individual. Emyr Lewis or *Tarw* ('the bull'), as he was affectionately known, had all the attributes listed above, and more. But what made him extra special was his attitude: he couldn't bear to lose!

There are some players who draw inspiration from their captain's pre-match team talk, or the hype in the press. Not Emyr. As soon as he put on his kit, he was ready for action, and there would be only one satisfactory outcome as far as he was concerned – a win! Once on the field, Emyr could be seen charging around after his opponents (hence the nickname), making tackles, creating effective platforms from which his fellow players could launch attacking moves and, more subtly, offloading telling passes.

Among many outstanding performances for his country, one in particular stands out. The game was in Cardiff in 1993 when England were on the brink of winning a third consecutive Grand Slam and started the match as clear favourites. But they hadn't reckoned with the defiance and dexterity born of Welsh desperation.

Now Emyr was lauded for many outstanding qualities as a No. 8 forward, but deft kicking hadn't previously been one of them. However, after stealing the ball from right under the noses of the old enemy, Emyr then proceeded to deliver a kick of which Maradona or Cruyff would have been proud. The ball bisected the defending three-quarters, and in an instant Ieuan Evans, who had left Rory Underwood in his wake, managed to get a right boot to the ball. It was then just a question of controlling the Gilbert and claiming a match-winning score. The whole of the Welsh nation (along with the late Princess Diana who was sitting in the front row of the South Stand) was on its feet in admiration and appreciation.

Tarw had become a tinker! He had been cheeky enough to steal the froth from the top of the Guinness – and this at the expense of the English!

Emyr Lewis: *Tarw* ('the bull').

41

Phil and Bryn

Fulfilling dreams

When we visit the cinema to watch the latest blockbuster, it is invariably (and inevitably) the star's name that is emblazoned on the screen – and only at the very end of the film will we see the list of people credited with putting the whole project together. The back pages of our newspapers are equally preoccupied with the stars of sport, with the extravagant talents of the Peles, Tendulkars and Jordans of their world. Or in rugby terms, with the Ieuans, Jonathans and Phils, whose mazy runs and amazing tries have brought specatators to the edge of their seats.

But how often do we acknowledge the hard graft put in by the eight forwards? After all, without possession from scrum, line, ruck or maul, the most gifted centre or wing three-quarter is no more threatening than a Terracotta warrior.

Llanelli RFC has always been proud that words such as 'flair', 'finesse' and 'panache' have all been synonymous with its style of play – and that style depends on the contribution of fifteen men, not on a handful of headline heroes. But where are the gratfers in my chronicle of Stradey's glories? Where are Edgar Morgan, Iorwerth Jones, Alan James, Alun Davies, Phil Davies, Julian Williams and their likes in Llanelli packs of the past? And what of Elvet Jones, Handel Greville, Bill Clement, Gwyn Ashby (the best executor of a dummy pass since William Webb Ellis started running with the ball), the British and Irish Lion, Peter Morgan and Bryn Howells?

There is an interesting anecdote involving Bryn Howells and George Nepia. As a young lad, Bryn had watched in awe as the All Blacks defeated Llanelli at Stradey during their 1924 tour. From that day on, his sporting hero was without doubt the legendary New Zealand fullback. Imagine Bryn's feelings years later when, as a member of the Belle Vue rugby-league team, he would take on a Streatham and Mitcham side that starred the same George Nepia. Bryn Howells was also an accomplished cricketer, playing in the Lancashire League against such luminaries as Sir Learie Constantine, Sir Frank Worrell and Dusty Rhodes.

One who played out his entire rugby career at Stradey Park was the second-row forward Phil May. A popular captain and perennially consistent player, Phil was physically strong at scrummage, ruck and maul. He was also a talented line-out jumper, either taking the ball at the front of the line and driving on with purpose or skilfully deflecting it back to his scrum half.

International honours came late to Phil – he was 31 years of age when he won his first cap for Wales at Twickenham in 1988. That season proved to be an unforgettable one. Having convincingly seen off England (thanks to a brace from Adrian Hadley), Wales beat the Scots at Cardiff (a spectacular try apiece for Jonathan and Ieuan). Paul Moriarty's try in Dublin secured a third victory and a Triple Crown. Everything now depended on the crunch game against France in Cardiff. Unfortunately, Wales played well below par and France won the match by 10 points to 9 – thanks to two penalties from Jean-Baptiste Lafond and a try by Jean-Patrick Lescarboura.

Whilst most of those present left the ground feeling despondent after coming so close to a Grand Slam, Phil May could at least feel some degree of contentment. After all, in the twilight of his rugby-playing career he had realised his childhood dream: he had won a cap. What is more, he had been part of the first Welsh team to win a Triple Crown for almost ten years.

Phil May, on the right, stealing the ball from a Cardiff line-out.

42

Ian Jones

Motoring à la TGV

It was during the summer of 1992 that I first encountered the exhilaration of travelling in that feat of French engineering, *Le Train à Grand Vitesse* – the TGV. With fellow members of staff, I was taking a group of schoolchildren from Pontardawe and Thouars on a day trip to Paris. As soon as we boarded at Poitiers, I knew that this would be a special experience for us all. The children were quickly ushered to their seats and we actually left the station on time!

Despite the fact that we were hurtling along at 185mph, it was easy to relax and watch the scenery flash by as the train snaked its way through the French countryside. Two hours after boarding we arrived at *Gare Montparnasse* in the centre of the capital city, all set to appreciate its unique history, architecture and ambiance.

A few weeks later, visions of the TGV came to mind as I was watching the final of the SWALEC Cup at Cardiff. The teams in contention that year were Pontypool and Llanelli and it was the skills shown by the Scarlets fullback, Ian Jones, which reminded me of the *Grand Vitesse*. In what I believe is one of the finest tries scored by a player in a Scarlet jersey, Jones gathered the ball on his own 22-metre line, and some 80 metres from the Viet Gwent try-line.

After juggling the ball in the air for a few seconds, he pirouetted on the spot and then with a sudden change of gear, he was off. The Pontypool players tore across the field in an attempt to restrain the Llanelli fullback, but their efforts were to no avail. Sidestepping off both feet in turn, he swerved past the Pooler defenders only to realise that he was perilously close to the touchline. It was now vital to regain his equilibrium whilst at the same time retaining momentum if he was to gain any more ground. Having accomplished both movements successfully, there was now the small matter of a 40-metre dash to the try-line.

Two questions hung on everyone's lips. Would his legs carry him the distance? Would his lungs survive the exertion? He had already overcome fifteen Pontypool players but everything now depended on his ability to overcome those last 40 metres. Visions of Ian Jones being stretchered off the field with an oxygen cylinder in tow were quickly erased as the fullback dived over the try-line close to the uprights! Had anyone suggested that he wouldn't make it? Never in Europe!

Ian Jones played at Stradey Park at the beginning of the 1990s. He showed great promise as a young man, and there were high hopes that he would one day represent his country. Unfortunately for him, although he came very close to winning a cap, he never managed to gain the ultimate prize. An American commentator once wrote, 'I'd love to borrow Muhammad Ali's body for 48 hours as there are three guys I'd like to beat up and four women I'd like to make love to.' Well, on that afternoon at the National Stadium, Ian Jones 'borrowed' Martin Offiah's speed, Mark Ella's cunning, and the precision of a Rolex timepiece. Ian Jones – musician, enigma and would-be TGV!

The flying fullback, Ian Jones.

43

Ieuan 2

The Scarlet Greyhound

Simon Barnes in his column in *The Times* wrote an interesting piece entitled 'The Maestros' with references to such sporting icons as Roger Federer, George Best and Muhammad Ali. To try to illustrate what set these people apart he recounted two stories. The first referred to a young, but gifted pilot who was learning the ropes from one of the more senior members of the air force. With just a few short weeks of training completed, the youngster left the more experienced pilots aghast as he completed a perfect landing at the first attempt.

The second tale involved a hugely respected music teacher who in a fit of anger and frustration shouted at his pupil, 'Go away! I can teach you nuzzink! From you I only learn.' If the pilot and pupil are the yardsticks, then it is obvious that there was more than the touch of a maestro about Ieuan Evans.

Before entering a foreign country, the traveller is asked to provide certain items of information regarding their identity, date of birth, address, reasons for visit etc. More often than not there is also a box marked 'occupation'. This part of the questionnaire can often prove to be a headache – but not for Ieuan. For him the answer is easy: 'Try scorer'. He was an expert in this department, and the list of tries he created and scored is a very, very long one. He was a right wing *par excellence.*

Ian Smith, Peter Jackson, Ken Jones, John Kirwan, Tony O'Reilly, David Campese, Jan Engelbrecht, Joe Rokocoko, Gerald Davies, Jonah Lomu, J.J. Williams, Patrice Lagisquet, David Duckham, Rupeni Caucaunibuca, Bryan Habana – some of the world's finest ever wing three-quarters, and in their midst, Ieuan Evans.

In a glittering career, Ieuan won 72 caps for his country, was captain on 28 occasions and scored 33 tries – and this in a period when the team was performing well below par and experiencing many an *annus horriblis*. In his role as captain, Ieuan refused to capitulate in the face of some stern criticism from the press, commentators and public alike. He was always most supportive of his players and never failed to encourage them – even when they had suffered yet another heavy defeat. He instilled in his team a sense of pride which bore fruit on that day in Cardiff on February 6, 1993 when they faced England in a vital Five Nations Championship match. It may have been Emyr Lewis's kick that began the move but it was Ieuan's lightning speed and his ability to control the ball that brought the try and with it a magnificent victory.

England were quite clearly the bookies' favourite to win at Cardiff and secure their third consecutive Grand Slam. It is true to say that most people in

Occupation: try scorer!

Wales thought that England would win – even the most die-hard supporters at Brynaman Rugby Club gave an eve-of-match prediction that there would be twenty-five points between the two sides and that Wales would come away as losers.

Small wonder, therefore, that Will Carling and his men were quietly confident when the scoreboard read: England 9 Wales 3. It was at this point that Emyr Lewis produced that now famous kick. At first it seemed quite an innocuous move and players and supporters alike just assumed that Rory Underwood, the England left wing (and RAF fighter pilot) would get to the ball and clear his lines.

But everyone reckoned without Ieuan's speed and determination. In a flash, he had passed Underwood and with a kick *à la* Michel Platini, aimed for the try-line. Suddenly the crowd, which had hitherto been in a state of suspended animation, sprang to life as everyone realised the impossible possibility of a winning try. If Jonathan Webb could be beaten, Ieuan had a clear run to the try-line. And this is of course what happened. Ieuan's turn of speed again came to the fore, the score was secured and Neil Jenkins's conversion sealed the victory.

The Welsh poet and Chaired Bard Myrddin ap Dafydd was moved to write a verse singing the praises of his hero after witnessing the event:

. . . Un am un yw'r ras	A rare one-to-one race
a ddihuna'r holl ddinas,	waking, exciting the city,
ysgwydd wrth ysgwydd 'wasgant,	neck-and-neck,
garddwrn wrth arddwrn yr ânt.	knuckle-to-knuckle.
Daw milgi Llanelli'n nes,	The Scarlet greyhound bounding,
mae'i wyneb lawn stêm mynwes,	his face full of steam,
mae'i holl einioes am groesi	his core full of scoring,
a myn diawl, mae'n mynd â hi!	and damn it, yes, he's done it!
Mae'n creu lle, mae'n curo'r llall,	He makes space, he beats his man,
yn seren ar gais arall.	the star of another score.

Some months before the game against the old enemy, Llanelli had played host to Australia at Stradey Park. All of the Wallaby big guns were on display for this match – Roebuck, Little, Horan, Kearns, McCall, Wilson, Eales, Gavin, Ofahengaue and Crowley. The Scarlets realised that they needed to be at their best and would need more than a little degree of luck if they were to overcome such a powerful unit. Thanks to two drop goals from the boot of Colin Stephens and yet another spectacular try from Ieuan Evans, Llanelli beat Australia by 13 points to 9. Among many notable wins and performances by the Scarlets, this ranks with the best ever.

There is a certain irony in the fact that the move that led to the try was one 'borrowed' from the Australian manual. During their 1984 tour of Britain, Australia had employed this move to great success on more than one occasion.

It involved the outside half Mark Ella feigning a scissors movement with his outside centre before passing dexterously to his fullback, Roger Gould. This caused such confusion in the opposing defences that it left a clear path for the attacker to run in for a try. Allan Lewis, the Llanelli backs' coach, having been impressed by this tactic (wing Phil Lewis benefiting from it in a Cup match during season 1985/86), had spent many a coaching session perfecting the same, and it was decided to use it against the Wallabies in the 1993 encounter! The gamble paid off handsomely. Colin Stephens and Simon Davies made as if to perform a scissors movement which allowed Ieuan to steam through the defence for the try. The Wallabies were well and truly fooled.

Before his retirement, Ieuan's last two seasons were spent at the Recreation Ground at Bath where he enjoyed another success as a medal winner in the prestigious Heineken Cup. The final was played at Stade Lescure in Bordeaux where Bath defeated Brive 19-18. To date Ieuan is one of only eight Welshmen to have appeared in a winning Heineken XV, the others being Tony Rees, Richard Webster, Nathan Thomas, Alan Bateman, Andy Newman, Robert Howley and Gareth Thomas. Would that a whole squad of players from West Wales could emulate this experience!

Ieuan's impact on a game of rugby cannot be overstated. Many is the time that the Llanelli faithful were seen streaming away from the ground on a cold winter's night in inordinately high spirits despite a dour performance from the team. The reason for the elation? A scintillating run or a breathtaking swerve from Ieuan was enough to set the scene alight. On one occasion the match was so dreary that a voice was heard to complain, 'Good grief, Cadbury's have got better centres!' But then Ieuan would enter the fray, and everything that had gone on before was forgotten. Ieuan Evans – a maestro!

44

Scarlet scrum halves

Skill and vision

Consider the following list of names: Evan James, Dickie Owen, Haydn Tanner, Rex Willis, Terry Holmes, Gareth Edwards, Robert Jones, Robert Howley, Dwayne Peel. These players are among the best scrum halves the nation has ever produced.

Now consider the following question. How many Llanelli scrum halves have won more than four Welsh international caps? The answer to the above is just two – Rupert Moon and Dwayne Peel, with Dwayne the only one to have won more than 25 caps. Onllwyn Brace played in eight internationals but only four of his caps were won whilst wearing the scarlet shirt of Llanelli.

During his playing career, Onllwyn Brace was considered to be the Frank Lloyd Wright of the rugby world – ahead of his time. According to Carwyn James, in terms of vision and understanding of the game, Onllwyn was 25 years ahead of his time. The following translated extract is taken from *Crysau Cochion*, a book published in 1958 and edited by Howard Lloyd:

> Onllwyn's unique contribution was not only his strength of character, but also his ability to bring a sense of adventure to the game. His main focus was on the scissors movement with its sudden change in the direction of attack. When his rather unorthodox movements didn't work, his team-mates were not unnerved, but were quite confident that a more orthodox approach would soon follow. We, in Wales, should be proud that this Welsh player is primarily responsible for the renewed interest and excitement generated in rugby circles during the period.

Onllwyn Brace.

Among many other first rate number 9s to have donned the Welsh jersey are Handel Greville (1947), Wynne Evans (1958), Mark Douglas (1984), Jonathan Griffiths (1988/89) and Michael Phillips. Two others who would have undoubtedly represented their country had they been born in

England, Scotland, Ireland or France were Dennis Thomas and Selwyn Williams. There are those Stradey stalwarts who would argue that Dennis Thomas was the best scrum half ever to have played for Llanelli. Dennis was the Terry Holmes of his day. As well as being physically strong, he could deliver a quick, accurate pass and he was

Dennis Thomas.

also fleet of foot – some of the credentials needed to become an effective scrum half. His other strengths were his ability to intimidate his opponents and create havoc in the opposition back row, ensuring that they needed to give him their full attention for the duration of any game. At a time when his game was beginning to blossom, and attracting the attention of the national selectors, Dennis Thomas's career was cut short due to a series of crippling injuries.

Selwyn Williams.

Apart from a brief period when he played with Ray Hopkins, Phil Bennett's scrum-half partner at Stradey Park was the indomitable Selwyn Williams. Selwyn's career at Llanelli lasted for over a decade, during which he played a major role in the team's success. He was like a terrier around the base of the scrum, always on the lookout for an opening and always a thorn in his opponents' side.

His pass, like that of Dennis Thomas, was like a missile, and like Dennis, he too was a fierce competitor. He refused to be intimidated and was often seen to tackle an opponent twice his size, indeed some players were upended as if they were unwittingly part of a judo competition.

The Eighties and Nineties saw the arrival of Mark Douglas, Jonathan Griffiths and Rupert Moon. Rupert defected to the Scarlets from his former club Neath when he was unexpectedly, and unfairly overlooked for a cup final encounter in the early Nineties. Despite a highly successful season at the Gnoll, Rupert was replaced at scrum half by Chris Bridges. Nevertheless, Neath's loss was Llanelli's gain, and Gareth Jenkins's faith in his new player resulted in the formation of a new confident, formidable unit. There are the

Rupert Moon.

purists who would argue that his pass could have been swifter. However, if this was a slight weakness, then it was counterbalanced by many strong points. Many thought that he played like the fourth member of the back row and this interplay between him and the forwards often paid dividends. He was also deceptively quick off the mark, and relished the prospect of causing mayhem among the opposition back row. He was often compared with *le petit général*, Jacques Fouroux. Of course any reference to the latter would elicit a quick response from Rupert – 'less of the *le petit*; more of the *grand général.*'

Rupert Moon is nothing if not a charismatic character. Inspite of his lineage (he was born and brought up in the Midlands), he has succeeded in winning over the heart and minds of the Stradey faithful and the Welsh public alike. His tenure at Llanelli was a successful one during which he won 24 caps for Wales, his adopted country.

Jonathan Griffiths is another player who made a remarkable impact during his time at the club. His move to St Helens to play in the professional ranks of rugby league also brought him a degree of additional recognition and success. He was an important team member when the Saints won the Rugby League Challenge Cup Final in 1996 (the first time for twenty years), playing a significant part in the 40-32 victory over Bradford Bulls. It has since been described as one of the best ever finals. Again it was his speed, agility and strength which made Jonathan such an invaluable member of the Scarlets and the Saints.

Jonathan Griffiths.

> Try for a goal that's reasonable and then gradually raise it. That's the only way to get to the top.

The words of Emil Zátopek, the 5000m, 10000m and Marathon Gold Medal winner at the 1952 Helsinki Olympics. This was the philosophy to which he himself aspired and which was also illustrated in an edition of the BBC television programme *Panorama* screened in the late Fifties and concerned with the rebuilding of Coventry Cathedral. The original building had, of course, been razed to the ground by the German Luftwaffe during the Second World War. There was now a vigorous rebuilding programme in place and several of the workers involved were questioned as to their role in the process.

The question posed was, 'What exactly is your job?' 'I have to trim the stones before carefully laying them in order,' was one reply. Another answered, 'I'm just following the architect's instructions.' The answer from the third craftsman was a revelation: 'I'm going to spend the next few years building a great cathedral.' Here was a gentleman who had a grasp of the bigger picture, and who was aware that he was part of an extraordinary event.

Herein lies Dwayne Peel's strength. He is another who has a vision; he is determined to succeed at the highest level. Now that he has starred in a Grand Slam campaign for his country and was one of a very few team members who returned from New Zealand with the British Lions with his reputation enhanced, Dwayne is beginning to realise this goal. There is one person who would have been tremendously proud of his grandson, and that is the late Bert Peel, who was for many years the first-aid man at Stradey.

Dwayne Peel was born and brought up in the village of Tumble in the Gwendraeth Valley. His early playing career was nurtured by his sports master, John Beynon, at Maes-yr-Yrfa School. Even though he now earns a living as a professional rugby player, Dwayne is still an eager student of the game. Interestingly, his mentor at present is the former Swansea, Wales and British Lions scrum half, Robert Jones. While he possesses all the attributes required of a modern day No. 9, Dwayne does not see himself merely as a link in the team; he has that extra dimension which enables him to vary attacks, and is often to be seen running menacingly from short penalties where his pace, penetration and persistence is often lethal. He is a creative force not to be underestimated. A Peel forage has a palpitating effect on spectators.

As with Haydn Tanner and Gareth Edwards before him, Peel's deadliness (as expresssed by Gareth Williams and Dai Smith in *Fields of Praise*) lies in its timing, its infrequency, its economy and its total success. He must be watched, patrolled and policed from kick-off to final whistle. Like a bottle of fine wine, the young scrum half's standard of play is maturing with age – we look forward to many vintage performances!

Dwayne's deadliness!

45

Five good and faithful servants

Classy centres

Class! A word used in many contexts to describe the indescribable. There are many stars of the silver screen who might be described as good-looking, charismatic, suave etc. but only a very select few are 'classy'. Sophia Loren, Audrey Hepburn and Grace Kelly are names which immediately spring to mind, together with that other icon, Jacqueline Kennedy Onassis.

Now, while Nigel Davies, the Scarlets' coach and former player would not take kindly to being listed with these ladies, he can nevertheless be deemed a 'classy' player.

Nigel Davies.

My first glimpse of Nigel's playing talents was at the Brewery Field, Bridgend. That day he was a schoolboy outside half, representing Wales Under Fifteens against the South of Scotland. As the match referee, I was able to study at close quarters Nigel's burgeoning talent. Even at such a tender age, he stood out; it was obvious that he had that extra 'something'. Here, certainly, was a player for the future. Some two years later, I would again witness a masterful performance when this time he played for the Welsh Youth XV at the Gnoll.

To the adjective 'classy' can be added 'slick' since his handling skills and timing of the pass were second to none. His favourite ploy was to draw his man and then, just as he was about to be tackled, hand on the ball deftly to his fellow centre. This ensured the continuity of the move while at the same time flat-footing the opposition. It was little surprise, therefore, that Nigel Davies would become an international player of some standing.

David Nicholas.

Another gifted centre of his era was David Nicholas (Dai Nic to his friends). He too was a natural footballer, possessing a magical left foot and an innate desire to attack from any situation. He will be best remembered for that heart-stopping break he made in the match against the Maoris at Stradey in November 1982.

With ten minutes left to play, the Maoris were ahead by 9 points to 6. A superhuman Scarlet effort and an individual stroke of genius would be needed to overturn the score. A Herculean run from Ray Gravell was enough to kick start the movement. Dai, who was storming down the left wing, took the pass and made a dash towards the try-line. The All Blacks were ready for him, they were aligned ready for the tackle. In an instant, Dai altered the direction and sprinted straight across the field, completely wrong-footing the Maori defence.

Frantically looking to right and left, hoping to release the ball to one of his centres, Dai suddenly opted to pass to his counterpart on the right wing, Peter Hopkins. The latter ran in easily for the try and Llanelli won the match 16-9. This brought a seismic reaction from the crowd who rose as one in appreciation of such an audacious but effective piece of attacking rugby.

Martin Gravelle is another name to conjure up images of exciting back play at Stradey Park. A natural, attacking fullback (and sometime centre), he knew to the micro-second when to time a run. His positional play was first class, he was deceptively quick and after making the initial break, made the pass to his wing three-quarter look effortless.

If Barry John, Phil Bennett and Gareth Davies were the doyens of the right-footed kick, then Martin Gravelle was their left-footed

Martin Gravelle.

152

equal. Anyone producing a training DVD on how to kick with the left foot would do well to employ the full back from Denham Avenue as their model.

It is rumoured that there are traces of Bedouin blood coursing through the veins of another Llanelli centre, Dafydd James, so often has he roamed from club to club. Until recently a member of the London club Harlequins, British Lion Dafydd has this season returned to Stradey.

He, too, is a strong, fast centre three-quarter whose reading of the game ensures that he always seems to be in the right place at the right time. His record in the Heineken Cup has been exemplary: two tries at Bourgoin, a scintillating run followed by a try in the semi-final against Northampton, and important contributions which led to Mark Jones's tries against Gloucester. There are those who feel, however, that Dafydd James's talents were not fully exploited during his first spell at Stradey. The tactic of relying too heavily on the pack coupled with the interplay between scrum half and back row meant that the backs were often deprived of the ball – but that is another topic for debate!

Dafydd James.

The last two seasons have seen the rise of another star centre three-quarter at Stradey Park. It is said that one indicator of 'style' or 'class' is freedom of expression, without which there is no individuality. Matthew J. Watkins is certainly a player of 'style' and 'class'.

Both on and off the rugby field, Matthew J. is a bubbly, mischievous individual, and these traits are reflected in the way in which he plays rugby. For him, this is a game to be enjoyed, a refreshing philosophy in this robotic age, when every move, run and pass seems to be pre-planned in the training sessions.

He will be the first to admit that he only decides on his next move when he has the ball in hand. Sensing this, a hush will descend over the ground and his fellow players will be rooted to the spot, wondering what will happen next. It is this maverick approach that endears him to both coaches and crowds alike. (Though, it is rumoured that it is Matthew J. who is responsible for the newly-acquired grey hairs which have appeared in the neatly-coiffured heads of Gareth Jenkins, Paul Moriarty and Nigel Davies!)

Since its inception a hundred-and-twenty-five years ago, Llanelli RFC has produced several mavericks and players of the highest class. Therein lies one of the secrets of its success.

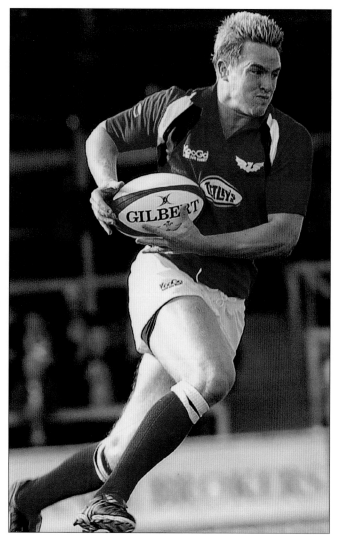

Matthew J. Watkins.

46

Jonathan

A phenomenon

Following my usual practice on a Saturday morning, I was enjoying my *latte* and turning through the pages of *The Independent Weekend Magazine*. As it was late July 2004, the television set was also turned on so that I could keep one eye on Brian Lara, who was at the crease batting for the West Indies against England. Whilst flicking through the pages, an article about the French ballerina, Sylvie Guillem, caught my attention. According to ballet critics, ballerinas of the calibre of Guillem only appear on the scene once in a lifetime. Such was her talent, that only a matter of days after joining the Opera Ballet School in Paris, the twelve-year-old Guillem was astounding her teachers. Her agility, poise and interpretation of the music was something at which to marvel. Years later, aficionados of the art recognise that Guillem has extended the boundaries of what is possible in classical ballet. In other words they regarded her as a phenomenon.

So, here I was reading about one phenomenon, watching another, and thinking what I was going to write about a third – the phenomenon of the world of rugby, Jonathan Davies. It is difficult to avoid using clichés, metaphors and the like when describing such a talented individual, suffice it to say that people like Guillem, Lara and Jonathan are unique – they aren't born every day! There is something in their genetic make-up that sets them apart. They are able to perform in a manner we lesser mortals can only wonder at.

During the early Seventies, I was on a mini bus travelling with a group of schoolchildren from Llandybie Primary School to Trimsaran where we were to face the might of the local school's rugby team. As we motored along in the Rees and Williams coach, confidence among pupils and teacher was high. Our record to date had been an excellent one; in fact we were unbeaten and were fairly certain that the afternoon's visit to Trimsaran would yield yet another victory.

Despite scoring four tries thanks to Stuart Griffith and Philip Lewis, we lost the match to a virtuoso performance by a ten-year-old boy wearing a white No. 10 jersey on his back. Now rugby pundits tend to categorise outside halves into two groups – the archetypal tall, lean-bodied, long-legged Englishman (although, admittedly, Jonny Wilkinson doesn't fit into this category) and the more squat, darting Welshman who flits around causing untold mayhem, which is Jonathan's group.

His performance at Trimsaran that Friday afternoon was a foretaste of what was to come: the look in his eyes, the way he handled the ball and of course

Jonathan – the master.

his magical sidestepping which was a pleasure to behold, even though we lost the match! As a schoolboy, Jonathan was a constant visitor to Stradey. His father Len Davies, himself a former Llanelli and Swansea centre three-quarter, would coax some life into the family Morris Minor as it negotiated the steep hill from Trimsaran to Llanelli. Phil Bennett and J.J. Williams were the young Jonathan's weekly heroes, but Boxing Day would bring him his Christmas bonus as London Welsh made their annual pilgrimage to Stradey. This gave him an opportunity to wonder at the skills of another hero, Gerald Davies, as he weaved his magic around the field.

Jonathan's first venture onto Stradey Park as a player came in 1981, when he was invited to take part in a trial match. He turned up, full of enthusiasm, but left feeling completely disheartened. Having been ignored by the coaching staff, he turned his sights east towards Neath and joined the set-up at the Gnoll. He spent the next five seasons playing for the Welsh All Blacks where he quickly made his mark and gained an army of adoring fans. There are those who still talk about the try he scored against the English champions, Bath. The game had been a hotly-contested affair with the result in the balance until Jonathan received possession from a centre-field scrum.

He feigned a drop-goal attempt, and then like a bullet sped past five if not six Bath defenders who resembled the proverbial rabbits caught in the headlights of a car. The headlines on the following day read 'Genius, destroyer, showman'. At the end of the 1986/87 season, relations between Jonathan and the Neath club became a little strained. The latter wanted him to commit himself to the club for the foreseeable future, but Jonathan was unwilling to agree to such a commitment. The result was that he returned to his old stomping ground at Stradey where he was to remain for just eighteen months before switching codes to play rugby league in January 1989. Jonathan's first six months at Llanelli were hampered by injury, but as he recovered, flashes of genius were again much in evidence.

Llanelli supporters would agree that his finest moment in a Scarlet jersey came in the 1988 Cup Final at Cardiff. Ironically, their opponents on that day were Neath and in that game Jiffy (as he is known) showed that he had yet another dimension to his repertoire. On his way to the match he received a card decorated with a Neath postmark. Thinking it was a good luck message from a friend, Jonathan opened it expectantly. A smile was soon wiped from his face when he realised it was from a few of his former 'friends' in the Neath squad. The picture on the front of the card was of the Llanelli team – but with a scribbled noose around Jonathan's neck and the letters 'R.I.P.' written underneath. They say that the prospect of imminent death concentrates the mind wonderfully, and this card seems to have done the trick for Scarlets' condemned man that day.

Neath were clear favourites to win the contest. Their pack had swept all before them throughout the season and, according to the pundits, Llanelli's only hope would come from utilising their talented back division. However,

The rugby Maradonas!
Phil, Barry and Jonathan playing soccer together for charity – in the black shirts of Neath!

without the ball in hand, this was not likely to happen. A superhuman effort from the Scarlets' forwards, with Phil Davies and Phil May playing the game of their lives, ensured that Jonathan had a steady supply of ball. Instead of adopting his usual tactic of darting and weaving all over the park, he resorted to kicking his team to victory. In true Cup Final fashion, the game was not a classic but none of the 57,000 strong crowd present would argue with the choice of Jonathan Davies as man of the match.

He left Stradey in January 1989 and joined Widnes Rugby League Club where he was to enjoy a glittering career in the professional code. The rugby-playing philosophy at Widnes suited Jonathan down to the ground – it was to run with the ball from all situations. Among many outstanding displays, the pinnacle of his career surely was the try he scored for Great Britain against the world champions Australia at Wembley. When historians record the greatest sporting moments at the old stadium then this try will rank amongst them. The list may include the gold medals won by Fanny Blankers-Koen in the 1948 Olympics; the genius of Stanley Matthews; Mortensen's goals for Blackpool against Bolton in 1953; Geoff Hurst's hat-trick for England in the 1966 World Cup Final; Ricky Villa's spectacular goal for Spurs in 1981 – and Jonathan's extraordinary try in October 1994.

As a commentator for S4C, I was fortunate enough to be present for this historic event. From our commentary position high up in the stands, we had an overview of proceedings and could see clearly how the various moves were developing. With Sean Edwards dismissed from the field after just 30 minutes of play, the game was building towards a dramatic climax. With just a few minutes left to the hooter, the score stood at four points apiece.

From this point on, I was no impartial commentator, as the atmosphere inside the ground was electrifying. Jonathan, playing at fullback, had the ball in his hands near the halfway line with thirteen Australians ready to rip him to shreds. In the post-match interview, conducted in Welsh in the tunnel area, the hero of the hour described to the viewers what happened next:

> To be honest, I didn't think there was a great deal on – the situation looked hopeless. I took the pass from Dennis Betts, and sensed there was a slight opening so I ran past the first defender, swerving on the outside to avoid two or three more. Unfortunately Brett Mullins, who as you know, is one of the fastest men in rugby league was waiting for the tackle. So, I slowed down for half a second, then bolted like a bat out of hell for the line. I realised that slowing down and then sprinting had him fooled. I've been lucky to be part of some fantastic moves during my career, but today, scoring a winning try at Wembley – that was something special.

Jonathan Davies, Sylvie Guillem and Brian Lara – three who unreservedly deserve the title 'phenomenon'.

47

S.Q.

The Q factor still a potent one at Stradey

It was the night before our daughter Lowri was born, and Jill and I were sitting in the back row of the Carlton Cinema in Swansea. These were the nearest seats to the exit, so that if she suddenly went into labour we could make a quick exit to Morriston Hospital. The reason for our visit to the art-deco cinema in Oxford Street at such a time was to see Jill's screen hero, Robert Redford, play the title role in *The Great Gatsby*. For her, and the countless numbers who enjoy American literature, there is only one Scott: *Gatsby*'s author, novelist F. Scott Fitzgerald.

Granted, there are several famous Scotts, but for those diehards who frequent the stands and terraces at Stradey there is no debate – there is only one Scott worth writing about, and that is Scott Quinnell. Born into an illustrious rugby-playing dynasty – his father Derek is a former Llanelli, Wales, Barbarians and British Lions forward, and his mother Madora's brothers are none other than Del, Barry, Alan and Clive John – it is small wonder that Scott ended up playing with an oval ball.

He fully lived up to the family name and could lay claim to a place in any team in any rugby-playing country in the world. What was it that made him so special? He was physically strong, a giant of a man, with the ability to consistently break away from set pieces leaving tacklers floundering in his wake. It usually took at least two defenders to bring him to ground thus creating spaces for others to exploit .

There were some armchair critics who, at one time, questioned Scott's commitment to the cause. They were soon silenced during the British and Irish Lions tour to Australia in 2001. Coupled with his physical presence was a natural sense of balance and ability to run with the ball in hand. This made him an extremely difficult opponent to play against. In February 1994, when he was just 21 years of age, Scott scored an incredible try for Wales against France at the National Stadium in Cardiff. From a line-out he picked up the ball by his bootlaces, flattened three pursuing Frenchmen and then stormed along the touchline to claim the try. This score went some way towards the total of 24 points the team amassed in their defeat of the *Tricolores* by 24-15. This was the first time in 12 years that Wales had beaten France and Scott played no small part in the victory.

Scott spent a short time at Wigan following in the footsteps of Ted Ward and Billy Boston. His early days at Central Park were difficult ones, but Scott's strength of character, grit and determination saw him develop into a very useful league player. He returned to Stradey when the union game turned professional and his riproaring appearances in the Scarlet jersey were a source of delight to the vociferous supporters who revelled in his charging, high-octane runs. There was no finer sight on a rugby field than to see Scott Quinnell breaking from a scrum, decimating the opposing defence, twisting and turning and more often than not ploughing over the try-line. 'Great Scott' – an apt title for one who succeeded in straining nerve and sinew for a worthy cause. His final season as a player also saw him coach Llanelli RFC to a Cup Final success against Pontypridd at the Millennium Stadium. Coach, television pundit, administrator . . .

We certainly haven't seen the last of Scott Quinnell; he fully deserves a place in the Stradey Hall of Fame.

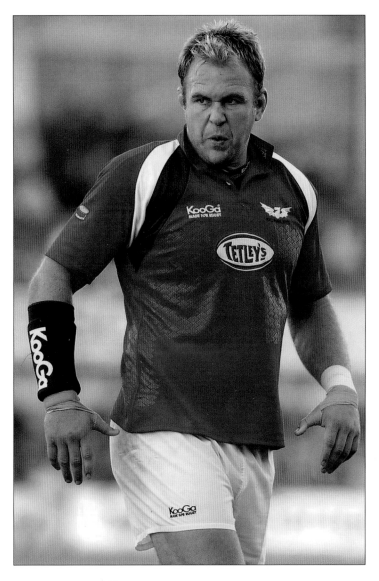

The destructive and creative No. 8.

48
Simon Easterby

Honorary Welshman

The Scarlet in the green jersey of Ireland.

The followers of Manchester United, Arsenal, Liverpool, Munster, Stade Toulousain and Llanelli all have one thing in common – they all support teams who play in similar colours. But that is where the similarity ends. Manchester United may have an Irish skipper in Roy Keane and Arsenal a French captain in Thierry Henry but such an honour is not generally granted at Stradey Park. Indeed, only a small nucleus of players from outside Wales has been adopted by the Llanelli faithful. Simon Easterby is one of the select few. Such is the high esteem in which he is held by supporters, players and administrators alike that he was elected captain for the 2004/05 season and for the current campaign.

A great honour indeed, especially when you consider that his formative years were spent over the border in England, Wales's arch rivals on the rugby field and all other fields! Simon and his brother Guy (who, until recently, was also a faithful servant of Llanelli RFC) were educated at Ampleforth College in the North East of England. This was also the alma mater of Lawrence Dallaglio and Bob Wilkinson. The young Easterbys soon came under the tutelage of former Harlequins, England and British Lions fullback, John Wilcox. As their talents matured, it came as no surprise that Clive Woodward, the national coach, tried to convince the two to wear the white shirt of England.

However, both Simon and Guy decided that their roots were firmly entrenched in the birthplace of their mother and they opted to represent Ireland at international level. Deciding which country to play for was not the only major problem young Simon had to face. In addition to being a rising star on the rugby field, he was also a promising cricketer coached by Don Wilson, the energetic and charismatic left-arm spinner who had represented Yorkshire and England in the Sixties and Seventies.

That he decided that his future sporting days would be spent playing rugby is a bonus for the Irish and Scarlets faithful who have witnessed some truly heroic and memorable performances. What, however, are his greatest attributes on the rugby field? There is his boundless energy and ability to play in any position in the back row. He is a fighter to the end with an innate ability to be in the right place to support the ball carrier and the vision to release team-mates at the exact time. There is an ever-present enthusiasm which is second to none and that stubborn determination to succeed which is embodied in the likes of Sir Steve Redgrave and Lance Armstrong. There was an interesting observation made by a pundit in a national newspaper recently who compared Simon to a barbed-wire fence: 'Thou shalt not pass!'

Alongside compatriots such as David Humphreys, Simon was forced to spend a few seasons in the international wilderness. This was a result of the international coach Eddie O'Sullivan's policy of maintaining a certain squad of players and not widening his horizons. However, with a great deal of hard work and no less patience, Simon Easterby has been well and truly at the forefront of the Irish team's success of late. His is the first name on the team sheets of both Ireland and Llanelli. What is more, though omitted from the ill-fated British and Irish Lions squad to tour New Zealand in 2005, he soon found himself flown out as a replacement, underlining the folly of coach Sir Clive Woodward's original selection, by forcing himself into the Test team on the back of some outstanding performances. For all the Lions' shortcomings, this must have been the icing on Simon's international rugby cake.

Off the field, Simon is an engaging personality, a young man who is not afraid to offer his opinion on a range of subjects. This is a refreshing quality in a professional sportsman where all too often the sole topic of conversation revolves around personal qualities and achievements.

This trait was exhibited at a family gathering just after the Irish team's return from the World Cup in Australia in 2003. I was interested to know what, from his point of view, had been the highlight of the competition. The answer, which was immediate, caught me unawares. It was the walk around the Adelaide Oval, the cricket-field venue for what proved to be a bruising encounter between Ireland and Argentina. Their previous World Cup fixture had been played at Lille in 1999, a match won by Argentina in the dying seconds when Diego Albanese crossed in the corner. This was their opportunity to exact revenge on Agustin Pichot's team – at least this was what I expected to hear.

To my great surprise and delight there was no mention of the oval ball on the vast campus that is the Oval. Indeed, the talk was all about cricket! While the other members of Keith Wood's team went to inspect the rugby area, Simon and Guy could be seen strolling quietly towards the cricket pitch. This was the stage on which Don Bradman had scored 299 not out against South Africa in the 1930s; the very surface where Rohan Kanhai had scored a century in each innings against Richie Benaud's star-studded XI in 1961. It was with a degree of awe and amazement that the two brothers stood on the pitch, soaking in the atmosphere and enjoying the moment. Without any prompting, Simon walked quietly to one end of the square and bowled an imaginary ball to his brother. Guy responded with some deft footwork which saw the same imaginary ball flying skywards towards the boundary!!

In that instant the two international rugby players had been transported back to their childhood and were now emulating their heroes of the past. The reaction of the remainder of the Irish squad has yet to be recorded!

Icing on cakes has already been mentioned in this piece – that was in a metaphorical sense. There was also icing on cakes in the summer of 2005 when Simon married Sarra Elgan, who is incidentally the daughter of former Wales and British Lions wing Elgan Rees. That accounts for Simon's presence in and around the Neath area – the Llanelli stalwarts need have no worries! It must surely follow that in addition to his loyalty to his Anglo-Irish roots, we can assume that Simon Easterby will also become an honorary Welshman!

49

Garan and Goran

Two of a kind

Garan Evans and Goran Ivanisevic – their names are not dissimilar and their careers have also followed a parallel course. The cronies of the tennis world would have us believe that the tall army officer from Croatia had had his day, his tennis career at an end. He was the player who promised so much but achieved nothing. During the 1990s, Goran had reached the semi-finals of several major tournaments, including Wimbledon, but had fallen at the last hurdle. Credited with having the fastest serve in the game, he endeared himself to tennis fans with his determination, warm heart and colourful personality. However, a fiery temper was often his undoing.

A catalogue of injuries during 2000 led to Goran missing several major tournaments on the tennis circuit and subsequently he did not merit an automatic entry to the 2001 Championships at Wimbledon. Devastated at his omission, he resolved to prove the authorities wrong. At the eleventh hour he accepted a 'wild-card' entry and arrived at SW11 on the first Monday of the Championship armed with a steely resolve to prove himself. 'Unfortunately, I always seem to come second. There is a degree of sympathy and respect out there, but from a personal viewpoint, coming second is just not good enough.'

During Wimbledon fortnight, Goran proved to those doubters, and primarily to himself, that he was a true champion. He reached the final yet again, but on this occasion he came away the winner, defeating the Australian Pat Rafter in five sets. It was a dream-come-true for the Croatian. Everyone – pundits, players, press, coaches and supporters alike – had written him off, but he had proved them all wrong. With sheer guts and massive self-belief, he had triumphed. He had not thrown in the towel.

This brings us to Garan. It was during the summer of 1998 that he received the invitation to travel with the Welsh team to South Africa. When he was eventually chosen to play in the Test match at Pretoria against the Springboks, Garan was elated. This elation, however, turned to despair when Wales were trounced 98-13 in a one-sided affair which proved an embarrassment for anyone who did not have South African blood in their veins. For many Welsh players involved in the massacre, the experience was too much to bear, and the international careers of many of them came to an end at Loftus Versfeld. For four long years Garan Evans's name was added to the list of one-cap wonders.

The years following his return from the African continent proved to be difficult. For a while, Garan (just like Goran) was beset with injuries. When he did resume playing, he realised that there was now stiff competition for the right-wing berth in the team. There were good, young players emerging and it was obvious he would have to work hard to regain his place. A lesser character would have yielded to the many pressures he now found himself under, but Garan was determined not to give in. The modest, red-haired flyer from Trimsaran proved that under that self-effacing exterior lies a backbone, resolve and dogged determination to succeed. The easy option would have been to walk away or to make waves and complain to the establishment and media, but that was not his way. Rather he took stock, persevered and made a decision to regain his place, initially at Stradey and then in the national side.

Garan is a 'Scarlet' through and through. Even in his darkest days when he thought that his playing career at Stradey was at an end, he rejected an invitation to join another club. He had been coming to Stradey from the time he took his first steps. It was always his ambition to play for the club, and it is here that he will see out his rugby-playing days.

Over the last seasons, Garan Evans has played some of the best rugby of his career. Whether it has been from fullback, or on the right wing, he has produced some scintillating performances; ones to match that unforgettable try he scored in the late Nineties at St Helen's in a match against the All Whites. Swansea were in a promising attacking position and had been camped in the Llanelli 22 for quite some time. Scott Gibbs had the ball in hand and supported by his forwards was about to launch himself at a tired-looking Llanelli defence. Somehow, the home side lost possession and in an instant Rupert Moon deftly flicked the ball to fly half Frano Botica who was positioned on the blind side.

In normal circumstances, a hefty kick towards Brynmill would have retrieved the situation but Botica, in true All Black and Llanelli fashion, decided to counter-attack. A magnificent fingertip pass released Garan, who was approximately 80 metres from the Swansea try-line. He had very little room to manoeuvre; the touchline was in close proximity and Mark Taylor was ready for the kill. However, the Llanelli wing three-quarter veered inside and then swerved outside leaving Taylor for dead. He was away. Despite being hotly pursued by half of Swansea, he was too quick for them and crossed for a truly memorable score right underneath the Swansea posts at the Mumbles end. Several superb tries have been scored at St Helen's over the years, and Garan's effort in that match must surely rank amongst them.

During the 2002/03 season he was justly rewarded for his performances. A second cap against Ireland in Dublin saw him scoring his first try for his country and he was also included in the Welsh squad which travelled to Australia and New Zealand. His inclusion in the party for the 2003 World Cup brought great satisfaction although his appearance against New Zealand resulted in disappointment when he was stretchered from the field in the opening minutes.

What has been responsible for this resurgence in confidence? The same qualities that enabled Goran Ivanisevic to win the Wimbledon crown – sheer guts and determination and the fact that throwing in the proverbial towel was never an option.

Twins Deiniol and
Garan – both of
whom have worn the
Llanelli shirt.

Another try for the
Trimsaran winger.

50

Northampton

Breaking the taboo

For the first two years of the new millennium one word was taboo in and around the streets of Llanelli, and that word was 'Northampton'. Over a period of several years, Scarlets and the Saints had faced each other in many bruising encounters – games which were still a topic of debate in the bars of the two towns.

Many former England internationals have represented Northampton: players such as Jeff Butterfield, a strong and creative centre with an instinctive side-step; the prop Ron Jacobs who had the physique of an ox, and the scrum half Dickie Jeeps who played in no fewer than three British Lions' series. These were all members of the Northampton team during the 1950s. During the 1960s two other British Lions came from the club, namely the back-row forward Bob Taylor and the wing three-quarter Keith Savage. Thus Northampton was not a team to be dismissed; it was a team with a distinguished pedigree, a team with the ability to nurture and develop young talent.

Any sense of mutual respect between the two clubs came to an abrupt end during the last week of April 2000. The match on this occasion was the semifinal of the Heineken Cup and took place at the Madejski Stadium in Reading. To this day there are still some Scarlet supporters who wake in the middle of the night as they relive the drama (or nightmare) of the occasion! There are others who blame the referee, while a third group point a finger accusingly at the coaches and blame them for employing the wrong tactics.

Whatever your point of view, Llanelli still lost the match. Northampton were the victors by 31 points to 28 thanks to an unbelievable kick from the accurate boot of Saints' outside half, Paul Grayson.

In the dying minutes of the game the score was level at 28 points apiece, and had the referee blown his whistle at that point, Llanelli would have won by virtue of the fact that they had scored more tries. However, the storybook ending was not to be. When Llanelli were harshly penalised, Grayson from a considerable distance took aim. A hush descended over the stadium. His preparations were meticulous. The ball torpedoed through the air, travelled some 50 metres before finally dropping over the crossbar. The supporters dressed in green, black and yellow were ecstatic while those in scarlet were dumbstruck in total disbelief. (Northampton then went on to win the Heineken Cup beating Munster at Twickenham by nine points to eight). That night, the convoy of cars and buses carrying the Llanelli supporters back down the M4 was a sorry one, as slow and lifeless as a funeral cortège. No one could believe what had happened. The team had played well, had come so close to winning, but fell at the last hurdle.

The 2003/04 season gave Llanelli an opportunity to gain some revenge over their old rivals as both had been drawn in the same group for the preliminary rounds of the Heineken Cup. Llanelli were the victors at Stradey, but they would have to triumph at Franklins Gardens if they were to reach the last eight of the competition. This situation had come about thanks to a splendid win by the Saints in Agen. Conditions for the match in France were atrocious. Vernon Cooper's team had experienced a taste of what these conditions were like a week earlier when the players felt as if they were playing in a vat of treacle, but when Northampton arrived things had deteriotated even further. Six inches of water in some parts of the ground compounded the situation, and it is somewhat surprising that the match was allowed to proceed. Be that as it may, the visitors won and now everything depended on the Scarlets' visit to Franklins Gardens.

For days before the match the press were hard at work hailing the encounter as 'Gunfight at the OK Corral'. For once a Welsh club was being afforded equal coverage with their English counterparts in the London press, not that any of them gave Llanelli a chance! To all intents and purposes this was an international and with England newly crowned as world champions, confidence in the English ranks was stratospheric. Everything pointed to a win for John Leslie's team: they were playing at home, they were previous cup-winners, and according to the press and the pundits, they were much the better team! One press report also foolishly declared that the Saints were undoubted winners as they played regularly in a Rolls Royce League whereas the Celtic League was more redolent of a Robin Reliant. Sales of *The Sunday Telegraph* plummeted in Wales after this article appeared!

As if all this was not enough, a column (this time in *The Daily Telegraph*) by the former England outside half Stuart Barnes incensed the Llanelli coach Gareth Jenkins. Stuart who is a well-respected writer and analyst pointed out that on two previous occasions Llanelli had come close to reaching the final and twice they had failed, losing in the final moments of both games. He questioned the tactics employed by the coaching staff and wondered if this had been a deciding factor and more to the point, would they get it right at the third attempt?

Tickets for the match were sold out within days, but a further disappointment was in store for the Stradey faithful when they realised that the club had been allocated just seven hundred tickets in a stadium with a capacity of over twelve thousand seats. Undaunted, the morning of the game saw all roads north to junction 45 of the M1 jammed with cars and coaches carrying excited supporters. Northampton, which had hitherto been famous for producing footwear (small wonder that Grayson succeeded with that mammoth kick), was now under attack from a Scarlet army.

As the match commentator for BBC Radio Cymru, I had arrived at the ground some hours before kick-off. The stadium at Northampton ranks as one of the best in Britain. Success on the field has resulted in redevelopment and rebuilding off it. Marketing is slick and the facilities available at this state-of-the-art campus second to none for playing staff, administrators and supporters alike. As I took in the atmosphere, I could hear the fans arriving. They were streaming in and in inordinately high spirits. The latest pop music was blaring out over the P.A. system, there were long queues at the club shop and the refreshment bars were doing brisk business. In the hospitality boxes, the hired help were checking on last-minute arrangements – Was the wine chilled? Did they have the cheque ready to pay the post-lunch speaker? The scene was set, and most people thought they knew what the outcome of the day would be.

And then something quite extraordinary happened. As I was checking my technical equipment, I happened to glance in the direction of the far touchline where I could see that the Llanelli squad had just arrived and were walking the hundred metres or so from the entrance to the changing rooms in complete silence. As they approached the dressing-room area there was an aura, a sense of total concentration; they were completely focussed, no doubts emerging,

The try of the season? The try of the decade?
Barry Davies's unforgettable score against Northampton.

possessing a self-belief and confidence for the impending battle. I knew in that instant that the Scarlets would win – as far as I was concerned the match was over even before the teams had set foot on the field!

And win they did, and with some style. In an exciting, closely-fought encounter, the Scarlets had much the better of their opponents apart for approximately ten minutes at the end of the first half. They also played their trademark game of fifteen-man rugby in a well-drilled, well-executed fashion. The first try was a classic: the ball was handled deftly between Scott Quinnell, Robin McBryde and Dafydd Jones with the Llanarth flanker being in the right place at the right time to claim the score. The second try had the crowd on its feet and is still discussed in the pubs and clubs around Llanelli (and, I dare say, even Northampton). Paul Grayson's kick was a gem, and nine times out of ten would have resulted in a Northampton try. But not on this occasion. Barry Davies, the Scarlets fullback, dived onto the ball in a style which would have pleased Greg Louganis, and then in one continuous movement got back onto his feet and sprinted like a hare for the try-line. The Saints' defenders were still freeing themselves from the mud when they realised that he had gone! Unbelievable! Incredible! Fantastic!

When the referee Donal Courtney blew his whistle to signify the end of the game, the scoreline was close but everyone present acknowledged that on the day the Welshmen fully deserved to win. To be fair to the Northampton supporters, they were gracious in defeat, and recognised that the better side had won. This sentiment was echoed by left wing Ben Cohen (he of 'Shane who?' infamy) who went over to the Scarlet supporters and warmly congratulated them on their team's victory. All is forgiven now, Ben, and we all knew that the Scarlets were the better side!

51

Perpignan

At least Lisa was still smiling!

Picture the scene if you can. Perpignan. Heineken Cup 2001/02. Eight tired, hungry reporters sitting around one of the tables in the Casa Sansa restaurant. As we eagerly awaited the arrival of the *soup à l'oignon*, the *Coquilles St Jacques* and the *Tarte aux myrtilles* washed down with a bottle of *Chateau Margaux,* I happened to glance around the room and my eye fell upon a face which seemed vaguely familiar.

He was a tall, dark-haired gentleman, and from his physique and demeanour, my companions and I decided that he must be a member of the Perpignan team. In hushed tones, we debated his identity and finally agreed that he must be the Argentinian forward, Rimas Alvarez Kairelis. Here he was on the eve of the big match enjoying a relaxing dinner with his very attractive companion.

All of a sudden another familiar face appeared at the restaurant door: John Thomas (John the Spy to his friends because of his connection with Eastern Bloc countries!), the referee and headteacher from Pontiets. He and a group of colleagues had made the journey from West Wales to Catalonia to support the Scarlets. After finishing my main course, I went over to John's table and having exchanged pleasantries he asked, 'Do you know who that is?' nodding in the direction of the Perpignan player's table. I told him that I did. But he had a second question. 'Yes, but do you know who the young lady is?'

'No idea,' I replied – this was quickly developing into a round of *Question of Sport.*

'That's Lisa – Lisa from Felinfoel. Born and bred within a Phil Bennett punt from Stradey, and they're courting.'

Now, Brynaman boys aren't backward in coming forward, so armed with this new information I made my way over to their table. After introducing myself, and after a polite *Buenas noches* in Rimas's direction, I then proceeded to interrogate Lisa about her family, her background and how the two had met – all basic questions that a good investigative journalist should ask! Their first meeting took place after one of the autumn internationals in Cardiff when Argentina played Wales – and yes, it was love at first sight. Fast forward to the present, and Lisa admitted that she had mixed feelings about the game. She would be going to Stade Aimé Giral wearing a Scarlet jersey and carrying a Catalan flag. Whatever the outcome she would be able to smile!

For all the warmth of the Catalan welcome in the town, the social pleasantries flatter to deceive: the exchange of banners, the handshakes, the polite nod of the head disappear like the morning mist once the whistle has blown. This also seems to be a signal for the bands to start up. They don't appear to play any particular tune, but the noise continues for a full two hours or more. Even the atmosphere in the state-of-the-art stands seems to change once the contest is under way. The smartly dressed Catalans suddenly become as intimidating and unruly as any rebel residing either side of the Khyber Pass. Little wonder that the Scarlets lost that day. And the time before!

Rimas in Perpignan colours against Toulouse.

What links Stade Aimé Giral, Donnybrook, Welford Road, Stradey Park, Thomond Park and Stade Ernest Wallon? Visiting teams don't win there, that's what. Therefore, when Llanelli welcomed Perpignan to Stradey Park for the 2002/2003 Heineken Cup Quarter Final, expectations for revenge were high. However, the overbearing tension proved too much for one member of the Llanelli XV, and he was dispatched from the field of play six minutes into the first half.

There would be no revenge that evening. Perpignan's Manny Edmunds inspired a Catalan victory that forced the Scarlets to put away the champagne once again and to drown their sorrows in the local Felinfoel brew. But amongst all the disappointed Scarlet faces, one young lady was smiling as her husband, Rimas Alvarez Kairelis, was in the winning team. If only he had been wearing Scarlet! I wonder who the twin daughters, Megan and Gwen, will support? Argentina? Wales? Or quite possibly, France.

52

Biarritz

No night out at the Ritz as the Scarlets lose out to the glitz

The Basque people are famous on many counts – they are *Cordon Bleu* cooks, they are master at *pelota* (reputedly the fastest ball-game in the world), they are brave (witness their running with the bulls at the annual fiesta in Pamplova) and they are agile and creative, as they demonstrate when they dance on glass. Despite recognising all of these talents, no one who lives west of Offa's Dyke saw them as a serious challenge to the Scarlets in the Heineken Cup match of 2003/04, especially as the quarter-final tie was being staged at Stradey Park.

On match day Stradey was in festive mood. An *al fresco* concert was in full swing with the traditional Basque brass bands entertaining the crowds, while the Welsh folk band, Jac-y-Do, were doing their bit inside the marquee. Everywhere one looked there was a sea of red and white (the Biarritz Olympique team colours) mingling happily with the scarlet of Llanelli. Every ticket had been sold and there was an air of expectancy. The Scarlets' supporters were aware that they had been badly let down a year earlier in a corresponding fixture against Perpignan, and were anxious not to witness a repeat performance.

When the teams took the field, it was noted that Biarritz were playing in their regional colours of red, white and green. They clearly regarded this as an 'international' match, and wanted to do their area proud. The opening minutes of the encounter proved a little tense; mistakes were made on both sides, and it was patently obvious that both sets of players were aware of the importance of winning a fixture of such magnitude. As the game progressed, Biarritz slowly but surely began to win more and more of the ball and this caused some concern in the home team defence. This degree of confusion gradually turned to panic as it became clear that Biarritz were stronger, faster and more street wise than they had been given credit for. As the teams left the field for the half-time interval the crowd was unusually quiet. It was as if everyone realised that this was a case of déjà vu, and the unthinkable was about to happen again.

Their worst fears were realised at the beginning of the second half when Nicolas Brusque went over for a try, and this during a period when their influential wing forward, Serge Betsen, was consigned to the sin bin. The supporters were now very uneasy and began voicing their opinions of the Scarlets' performance. Matters improved temporarily when Leigh Davies made an appearance as replacement, but this transient threat was soon negated when in the dying minutes of the game, Thomas Lievremont's team scored another two tries. The Scarlets had been well and truly beaten, the crowd filed home under a cloud of disbelief and frustration. It had been painful to see their team lose in such a clinical manner.

Two weeks earlier, the Scarlets' fans, and indeed rugby supporters across Europe, were questioning the decision of the Welsh Rugby Union not to appoint Gareth Jenkins as the national coach. Letters were written in the press and the subject was hotly debated in the media. Now, after such a defeat at the hands of Biarritz, some questioned Gareth's competence at the highest level. Some saw a defeat in the league as excusable; the situation could be resolved the following Saturday. To lose in a home quarter-final tie was a different matter altogether. This was a time for retribution; things were said in the heat of the moment and accusing fingers were pointed at the coaching staff responsible for the catastrophe. If a week is considered a long time in politics, then 80 minutes on a rugby field must have seemed like an eternity.

For many seasons the Scarlets had represented Wales with distinction on foreign fields. The Club, through the dynamism, expertise and motivational skills of Gareth Jenkins, had managed some memorable Heineken successes and had been unlucky in two semi-final performances at Reading and Nottingham. Clubs in England, Ireland and France were fearful of the Scarlets; the team from West Wales, as a result of the quality of their players and meticulous match preparations, proved difficult to beat. Stade Toulousain, Leinster, Leicester, Northampton, Munster, Sale, Bourgoin and Wasps were in awe of the club's impressive achievements.

The defeat at the hands of Biarritz was a wake-up call. The basic structures were in place but it was time for change. While no one doubts Gareth Jenkins's pivotal role in this new development, the club needs to invest time and money in the preparation of an efficient strategy and finalise long-term objectives in order to prepare for a healthier future.

Biarritz's international fullback, Nicolas Brusque, a thorn in the Scarlets' side.

53
Statistics

Llanelli Rugby Football Club

SEASON 1875/76 – SEASON 2002/03

POINTS IN A SEASON
Gary Pearce   420   1985/86

TRIES IN A SEASON
Carwyn Davies   45   1987/88

POINTS IN A CAREER
Andy Hill   2,577   1967-1979

TRIES IN A CAREER
Andy Hill   312   1967-1979

POINTS IN A MATCH
Colin Stephens   39   vs   Newport   19/09/92

TRIES IN A MATCH
6   Alby Evans   vs   Pembroke   01/03/1902
6   Ieuan Evans   vs   Merthyr   15/11/1986
6   Ieuan Evans   vs   Maesteg   24/10/1992

APPEARANCES
Phil May   552
Ivor Jones   552
Laurance Delaney   501

21 INDIVIDUALS HAVE SCORED OVER 100 TRIES FOR LLANELLI. THE FOLLOWING HEAD THE LIST:
Andy Hill   312   Ray Williams   213
Ieuan Evans   193

THE MOST COMPREHENSIVE VICTORIES:
106-0   vs   South Wales Police   12/03/1986
100-0   vs   Ynys-y-bŵl   13/02/1999

THE WORST DEFEAT :
3-81   vs   New Zealand   08/11/1997

01/01/1875 UNTIL THE END OF SEASON 2002/2003:
PLAYED   4,727   WON   3,022
LOST   1342   POSTPONED   5
DRAWN   358
WINNING PERCENTAGE   63.93%

54

Yes, surprisingly,
they also played for Llanelli!

A.B. (Arthur) Edwards (London Welsh and Wales). Two caps for Wales during season 1954/55. He represented the Scarlets during season 1948/49 whilst a student at Aberystwyth University. His grandfather hailed from Llwynhendy and desperately wanted Arthur to play for the 'best club side in Wales'. His first cap was gained against England at Cardiff on January 22, 1955. The match was postponed for a week as a result of adverse weather conditions in South Wales. During the training session at the Wanderers' Ground at Ely on the Friday morning, the vastly experienced Garfield Owen from Newport was injured. In those days, there weren't any replacements or reserves in attendance, and it was decided to get in touch with A.B. Edwards immediately. On the Saturday of the match, the ground was in a sorry state, reminiscent of a pot of glue, but this did not prevent A.B. succeeding with a straightforward penalty goal and this after ten minutes' play – the game's solitary score. This proved to be Bleddyn Williams's final international game.

Gerald Davies (Cardiff, London Welsh, Wales and Lions) Born and bred in Llansaint near Cydweli, Gerald played for Llanelli during his final year at Queen Elizabeth Grammar School, Carmarthen. When, however, he was invited to play on the wing against the 1963 All Blacks, he modestly declined, feeling that, as a centre three-quarter, he should not play instead of the club's regular wing three-quarters. During the early Sixties, the club experienced administrative problems – there was uncertainty regarding team selection, with players meeting for the first time on train platforms and in changing rooms. This inevitably resulted in inconsistent performances. The team's fifty-point defeat against Harlequins at Twickenham was the final straw; Gerald decided to join Cardiff RFC. A young player who became one of the world's greatest-ever players, born just eight miles from Stradey Park, and who had supported Llanelli on the Tanner Bank all his life, had to bid a sad farewell to his favourite team.

Ian Hurst (New Zealand). Season 1974/75 proved a rather historic one. The Scarlets were forced to play two matches on the same afternoon. Newport refused to release Phil Bennett's team from their arranged fixture, whilst the Welsh Rugby Union insisted that the Welsh Cup match, which had been called off the previous week as a result of bad weather, had to take place at the same time. Carwyn James, the Llanelli coach, took up the challenge selecting his strongest team for the Amman United (one of his former clubs) cup match, and with some assistance from neighbouring clubs and various individuals arranged for another Llanelli XV to travel to Rodney Parade. The select XV included New Zealand's star, Ian Hurst, and a Canadian international flank forward, Gordon Fownes. Hurst played for the All Blacks in the unforgettable 1972 match at Stradey, and readily agreed to help out both Carwyn and Llanelli. Apparently, the treasured Scarlet shirt is still in his possession!

Gareth Griffiths (Cardiff, Llanelli, Wales and Lions). In his excellent unputdownable volume *The Gwilliam Seasons*, the author David Parry Jones places Gareth Griffiths in the same category as Lewis Jones, Bleddyn Williams, Cliff Morgan and Ken Jones – individuals who had the capacity to change the course and direction of a match in an instant. Gareth and Bleddyn were the two Welsh centre three-quarters during Wales's historic triumph against the All Blacks in 1953. With half an hour remaining, Gareth dislocated his collarbone, but after receiving treatment he bravely returned to the action loitering out on the left wing for the remainder of the game. He flew out to South Africa in 1955 as a replacement and represented the Lions in the final three test matches. He joined Llanelli during the 1960/61 season.

Cliff Morgan (Cardiff, Bective Rangers, Wales and Lions). Yes, the great Cliff Morgan represented Llanelli on just one occasion, an honour the club will always treasure. In March 1958 the outside half was on his way to London to compère the Annual St David's Day Concert at the Albert Hall. When Cliff stepped onto the train at Cardiff Central Station he was enthusiastically greeted by members of the the Llanelli XV, or should I have said XIV. They too were on their way to the capital city to play the London Wasps but without their outside half Carwyn James. As a result of his early-morning teaching duties at Llandovery College, he had missed the train. Cliff was invited to deputise and, before the Pullman carriages had pulled into Newport station, he had reluctantly agreed to play. A message was sent to the concert's organisers who needless to say weren't too happy with the arrangement. The rehearsals went on as planned without the MC who eventually arrived in good time for the performance. Despite a display which earned him some compliments in the press, Llanelli still lost 11-9. He returned via taxi to the Albert Hall with a prized scarlet jersey in his possession and the pricely sum of £2 as expenses! Apparently the taxi ride was £5.

Gareth Evans (Cross Keys, Newport, Cardiff, Wales and Lions). Cross Keys agreed to release Gareth to represent Llanelli against Newport on the day when they had to fulfil two fixtures on the same afternoon. He partnered Ian Hurst in midfield and although the Scarlets lost by 23-4, the two centres combined well under the circumstances. Gareth was a dependable, intelligent three-quarter who represented Wales and the Lions with some distinction.

Brian Price (Newport, Wales and the Lions). It's true to say that Brian was to Newport what Ray, Delme and Phil were to Llanelli. Black and amber blood flowed through the veins of one of Wales's greatest ever second-row forwards. If he was Newport through and through, then how on earth did he come to play for Llanelli? The national selectors were responsible – Brian had to prove his fitness prior to a vital international and Llanelli agreed to include him in their starting line-up against Bridgend at the Brewery Field. Bizarrely, the Scarlets omitted Delme Thomas who would have played for Wales had Brian failed to complete the match. By the way, Brian still treasures the experience. He has always been an admirer of Llanelli's style of play.

John Gwilliam (Cambridge University, Edinburgh Wanderers, Gloucester and Wales). 23 international caps, and Welsh captain during their successful Grand Slam campaign 1949/50. Remarkably, not one Llanelli player was included in the squad as Lewis Jones was registered with Devonport Services. Gwilliam was an inspirational leader, and the Scarlets could testify to that fact after he played his one match (scoring one try) for Llanelli at Stradey against Bristol in January 1952. The reason for this one appearance? His wife was born and bred in the town.

Ian Allan Alexander MacGregor (Scotland). Born in Glasgow, the back-row forward spent a season at Stradey after receiving a Commission with the Royal Air Force. He won 5 of his 9 caps for Scotland whilst based at Pembrey. During season 1955/56, Ian and R.H. Williams were the only Llanelli representatives in the international arena. He was an aggressive, highly-respected forward and interestingly in one international programme at Murrayfield, an union official had included the following sentence: 'His form in recent trials suggested he has not been wasting his time at notorious Stradey Park!'

Clive Rowlands (Pontypool, Swansea and Wales). The majority of Welshmen associate Clive with Pontypool and Swansea. However, it was at Stradey that he was introduced to the first-class scene mainly at scrum half, although the Cwmtwrch cavalier insists that there were many fine cameo performances at centre three-quarter. The journey from Cwmtwrch to Llanelli for the weekly training sessions proved just as difficult as that from Moscow to Vladivostok – a James bus to Ammanford, a Rees and Williams coach to Llanelli town centre followed by a brisk walk across People's Park to Stradey. *'Ar ôl newid, rwbo'r* wintergreen *ar y coesau, ro'dd hi'n amser dala'r bws d'wetha nôl.'* Clive's words – after changing and rubbing on the wintergreen, it was time to go home!

The period was an exciting one: young, talented footballers came to Stradey solely to learn from the master exponent of scrum-half play, Onllwyn Brace. Clive became one of only a handful of players to have captained his country

179

whilst winning his very first cap – a great honour. His finest hour was leading his country to Triple Crown success during season 1964/65; two other Llanelli stalwarts shared in the honours, Terry Price and Norman Gale.

Clive captained West Wales in a memorable match at St Helen's, Swansea in 1967 against Ian Kirkpatrick's All Blacks. The combined side came within a whisker of defeating one of the finest New Zealand teams to have visited these shores. Clive controlled play effectively, and cleverly created two tries for the Neath wing three-quarter, Hywel Williams. Unfortunately, both were disallowed by referee Mike Titcomb; Hywel being ruled off-side on the first occasion and Clive's pass inexplicably deemed a forward one on the second. Two Llanelli players represented West Wales on that glorious afternoon – Byron Gale and Delme Thomas.

Alan Rees (Maesteg, Leeds and Wales). Alan served an apprenticeship at Stradey before joining Maesteg. A classical outside half, ghosting through openings and constantly breaching defences. He turned professional, joining Leeds Rugby League Club before returning to Wales and embarking on a highly successful cricketing career with Glamorgan. A talented batsman and a truly outstanding cover-point fielder often compared with Colin Bland, Paul Sheehan and Clive Lloyd.

One could go on and on, but where does one draw the line? Here are some others:

> P.Benka-Coker (Rosslyn Park), **John Currie** (Harlequins), **Allan Martin** (Aberavon), **Stuart Evans** (Swansea and Neath), **Rowland Phillips** (Neath), **Howell Davies** (Bridgend), **Arthur Emyr** (Swansea), **Mark Bennett** (Cardiff and Bristol), **Steve Moore** (Swansea and Narbonne), **Roland de Mirigny** (Italy), **Gavin Henson** (Ospreys).

Gareth Edwards's name appeared in two programmes published during season 1965/66. One of rugby's most famous sons was still a pupil at Millfield School when the invitation was received to represent the club in the Easter matches against Northampton and London Irish. Unfortunately, he declined the offer and opted to play for Cardiff.

If knowledgeable supporters were to sit down and select Cardiff Rugby Football Club's finest ever XV, then **Cyril Davies** and Bleddyn Williams would form an exceptional partnership in midfield. However, it was at Stradey that he embarked on his rugby career in October 1956. If one were to list the ten best centre three-quarters to have represented the national XV since the first international match in 1881, then Cyril Davies would be in the top five. Whenever he took to the field Cyril's performance was a masterclass in centre three-quarter play. As a passer of the ball he was in the same league as Phillipe Sella and Hugo Porta. He was one of six Llanelli players to play for Wales against Australia in 1958, the others being Terry Davies, Ray Williams,

Carwyn James, Wynne Evans and R.H. Williams.

In a trial match at Cardiff, before winning his first cap, an amusing incident took place. Playing for the Possibles, he created a glorious opening with a text-book outside break. His path however was blocked by his team-mate at Llanelli, the highly experienced Terry Davies, who was the Probables fullback. All Cyril had to do was to draw his man and release his wing three-quarter who would in turn race

Cyril Davies: on the right in the back row.

over for the try. In an attempt to help further his team-mate's career, Terry at the crucial moment shouted, *'Twl hi mas NAWR!'* – 'throw it out now!'

He played his final game for Wales against England at the Arms Park in January 1961. He created two glorious tries for Dewi Bebb (Wales won 6-3) before leaving the field early in the second period with a burst blood vessel. Unfortunately, at the age of 24, his career came to a premature end.

Other individuals whose careers blossomed at Stradey Park and who currently hold important roles at national and regional levels are the former talented back-row forwards, **Lyn Jones** and **David Pickering**. Lyn is Chief Coach to the Ospreys and David is a respected administrator with the Welsh Rugby Union. Another former Scarlet, **Keith Rowlands**, was appointed

President of the Welsh Rugby Union in September 2004. Keith played for Llanelli during the late Fifties, partnering the great R.H. Williams in the second row, before moving east to Cardiff. Keith also represented Wales and the British and Irish Lions.

The open-side wing forward, **Gwyn Jones**, spent a satisfying period at Stradey before joining Cardiff RFC. His medical studies at Cardiff meant that the constant travelling between Llanelli and Cardiff for practice sessions became too much and the move to join Cardiff RFC was unavoidable. Gwyn was an intelligent, athletic and creative back-row forward. His tragic accident deprived Wales of an individual who was developing into a player of the highest class. However, his determination to succeed in the face of adversity means that he is now making his mark as a respected and straight-talking commentator and journalist. His well-thought-out pieces in *The Western Mail* have been a breath of fresh air. Gwyn is always honest, controversial, unbiased and to-the-point. Viewers to *Y Clwb Rygbi* and *Scrum V* can still benefit from his excellent analysis.

Gustave Flaubert's main aim as a twelve-year-old boy in 19th-century France, was to leave Rouen and develop a career as a camel rider in Egypt, and then lose his virginity to a shapely, olive-skinned young girl in a harem in Alexandria. My dream as an innocent 12-year-old in the Brynaman of the early Sixties had three components: one was to represent Llanelli RFC, a second was to open the batting with Alan Jones (that dream was recently realised when I walked out with Alan at Drefach in a Robin McBryde Testimonial Match; unfortunately I ran him out after two overs), and the third was to defeat Rod Laver in a Wimbledon Final. Having achieved just one of these I am full of admiration for all those named in this chapter who have achieved so much more.

Keith Rowlands: the man in charge with his roots deep in Stradey soil.

55
Stars and Scorers

Carwyn Davies: one of the rare few to have scored over 100 tries for Llanelli – sharp, shrewd and speedy.

Salesi Finau: competitive and physical on the field, one of the most popular of Stradey's adopted children

Mark Jones: a bright talent

Wayne Proctor: over 100 tries for the Scarlets – a top winger.

Phil Davies: the accomplished No. 8 who has subsequently become a respected coach.

And the best team ever?

I couldn't sleep one night, so naturally I pondered which players from all those generations of Scarlets would best combine to create the perfect team.

This is my personal choice and you don't have to agree with it!

15 Terry DAVIES

14 Ieuan EVANS
13 Albert JENKINS
12 Ray GRAVELL
11 J.J. WILLIAMS

10 Phil BENNETT
 9 Dwayne PEEL

 1 Barry LLEWELLYN
 2 Norman GALE
 3 Tom EVANS

 4 Delme THOMAS
 5 R.H. WILLIAMS

 6 Derek QUINNELL
 8 Scott QUINNELL
 7 Ivor JONES

Testimony to the superb spirit that sustains the club.

Ricky Evans, the powerful prop.

Mark Perego: wing forward
and all-round action man!

Garan, Mark and Salesi in their element
after capturing the Cup, 2002/03

56

The Celtic League

Deserving of more respect

'A Mickey Mouse League'. Just one of the insults hurled at the Celtic League by the English press. Some say it is rather surprising that they were aware of its existence at all, such is the lack of broadsheet interest in anything that takes place on rugby fields west of the Severn Bridge.

The article in question appeared in the Sports section of *The Western Mail* on August 28, 2004. In it, Mark Evans, the Rugby Director at NEC Harlequins made the following comments: 'It is a second-rate competition. It is impossible to compare the Celtic League with the Zurich League in England in terms of finance, standard of play and crowd numbers.' Perhaps you are correct Mr Evans – even if the prickly pedants would remind you that your beloved Zurich (or, by now, Guinness) League struggles in comparison with the *Championnat* in France in terms of finances, competitiveness and spectator numbers! I'm just surprised that *The Western Mail* saw fit to give Mark Evans column inches, but then again maybe not.

Yes, of course there is room for improvement. The regional clubs are to be commended for insisting that their international players turn out for Celtic League fixtures. There is constant frustration when Leinster, Munster or Ulster travel to Newport, Swansea or Llanelli without the presence of players of the calibre of Brian O'Driscoll. It is also hoped that standards amongst Scottish clubs will rise in the future, and judging by Edinburgh's performance at Stradey in early September 2005, that might well be the case.

Perhaps Mr Harlequins should have completed some research and studied some statistics before he put pen to paper. During the past few seasons, Welsh clubs have done rather well against their English counterparts. Llanelli, Swansea, Neath, Pontypridd, Newport, Cardiff, Bridgend and Llanelli have all won both home and away in Anglo-Welsh contests. During season 2003/2004, the now defunct Celtic Warriors beat Heineken Cup champions Wasps at High Wycombe, the Scarlets beat Northampton both at Franklins Gardens and Stradey, the Ospreys defeated Leeds, and the Blues overcame Sale. Not bad for teams playing in a 'second-rate league'. And what about your team, Mark?

It would be foolish to deny that at the present time the Celtic League is on a par with the Guinness, but these are very early days. You have to walk before you can run. If the Celtic countries can act together in a responsible manner, who knows what can be achieved in a decade? And what if this season's Anglo-Welsh encounters prove nail-biting affairs?

Season 2003/04 saw twelve teams competing in the Celtic League. Because the World Cup was taking place in Australia, most of the international players were unavailable. As a result the participating teams had to depend on the younger, less experienced members of their squad or in some cases untried individuals, to help them out.

Occasionally, in the sporting world, an opportunity will present itself without much warning. This may be due to injury or a family crisis or illness. Whatever the reason, there are always those who, when given a chance, will step up into the breach and take full advantage of the opportunity afforded them. Geraint Jones, the Welshman who keeps wicket for England, is a prime example. When called up, he was told in no uncertain terms that he had one series to prove himself with the bat and gloves. He rose to the occasion, scoring a century to cement his place in the starting XI. The recent triumphant Ashes series saw Jones again under pressure from members of the press for his inadequate wicketkeeping but rebuffed his critics in some notable partnerships with Andrew Flintoff.

In 1988 Josiah Thugwane was discharging his duties as a gardener in South Africa. As he was going about his chores, a group of men from the nearby gold mine ran past the garden where he was working. Without a moment's hesitation, Josiah decided to join them on their run. Half an hour later, still in his gardening clothes, he decided that this was what he wanted to do with his life. Fast forward eight years and the world saw Josiah standing on the winners' rostrum at the Atlanta Olympic Games winning the gold medal in the Marathon. Similarly, several young Llanelli players won for themselves a professional contract as a result of their hard work and industry during the 2003/04 Celtic League Season. Proof of this was seen at Thomond Park, Limerick, where the Scarlets became the first visitors to defeat Munster at the venue since 1987.

With one game remaining, three teams were in the hunt for honours – Ulster, the Newport Gwent Dragons and the Scarlets. However, the Scarlets had a distinct advantage over their rivals: a victory over their Irish opponents in the crucial encounter at Stradey would see them crowned champions. It was an emotional evening; the supporters came in their thousands confident of success after the Biarritz disappointment. In an evening of high drama, they were not to be let down. There were moments of uncertainty as both teams realised what was at stake. The game's man of the match was undoubtedly outside half Stephen Jones, his personal tally of points proving absolutely vital. He left the field of play some five minutes before the final whistle to a tumultuous reception – his final game in a Scarlet jersey before his departure to France.

The Scarlets won the match by 23-16; five penalties and a dropped goal from Stephen Jones. He also played a major part in Matthew J. Watkins's solitary Scarlet try. Scott Quinnell and Iestyn Thomas were influential in the movement before Stephen's long pass was seized upon by M.J.W. The scenes at the end of play were reminiscent of Millennium Night celebrations. Stradey was a sea of scarlet, fireworks lighting the evening sky and everyone in festive mood. 39 players were involved during the campaign and everyone took to the field to acknowledge the warm reception.

However, during his after-match comments, Gareth Jenkins quite rightly concentrated on the high standard and committed performances of the fringe players. They had been primarily responsible for keeping the Scarlets in pole position. Their names should be recorded for posterity: Ian Boobyer, Gareth Bowen, Dale Burn, Lee Byrne, Aled Gravelle, Bryn Griffiths, Phil John, Richard Johnston, Emyr Lewis, David Maddocks, Gavin Quinnell, Richard Rees, John Thiel, Ceiron Thomas, Gareth Williams, Nathan Williams, Rhys Williams and Adam Yelland.

Winning the Celtic League – a chance to celebrate the whole squad's efforts.

57

Stephen Jones

Au revoir and bon voyage

Whilst driving along the M11 near Stansted Airport, I happened to tune in to a local radio frequency. The programme being aired was the usual mixed bag of music and chat, interspersed with the odd quiz question. As the broadcast drew to a close, the presenter played the perennial favourite 'What a Wonderful World', and invited the listeners to ring in and name the singer. Of course everyone knows that it was Louis Armstrong – everyone, it seems, except the gentleman who rang in with the answer. He was a little hesitant, so to help him claim his goody bag, the presenter thought she would help him along with some simple clues.

'Christian name. An American heavyweight boxer from the Thirties; first name Joe.'

'Yes' replied a voice at the other end of the line, 'I think I've got that.'

'A surname of two syllables. First syllable, a part of the body between your elbow and hand.'

'Fine'.

'And finally. If you're not weak you're...'

'I've got that,' came the confident reply.

'So who sang the song?'

'Frank Sinatra!'

I couldn't believe my ears. I was laughing so much I almost drove off the hard shoulder of the motorway. Where on earth was his common sense?

But common sense is exactly what has to guide the modern-day professional player who has an eye to the future. Like it or not (and many supporters don't), it is market forces which dictate where the best players will end up. Whereas in the amateur days, players remained commendably faithful to a particular club, nowadays it would be a foolish man who turned down a lucrative contract which would give him financial security way past his expected fifteen seasons as a professional player. In a parallel situation, consider a young solicitor working in West Wales. His or her hourly rate is £x. He/she is then offered a position in Bristol or Durham for £5x per hour. Can you honestly expect that individual to stay in Llanelli just because the town has a pleasant coastal path?

It is this dilemma which faced Stephen Jones when he was offered the opportunity of playing in France. To their credit, the Llanelli supporters, although obviously disappointed that he was to leave Stradey, understood his situation and showed their appreciation for what he had done for the club in his last match against Ulster and wished him further success at Clermont Auvergne.

189

It is always a temptation to compare and contrast the talents of players from different eras. In the past, Cliff, Phil, Barry or Jonathan, for example, delighted crowds from Cefneithin to Canterbury with the wizadry expected of the traditional Welsh fly half. Stephen's contrasting qualities have, however, made him an equally hot property in the modern game.

It is ironic that we in Wales did not really appreciate what Stephen had to offer until he had left and gone to play his rugby in France. In fact his contribution to the national team was occasionally called into question during the preliminary rounds of the World Cup in Australia in 2003. Yet when Wales enjoyed their renaissance against New Zealand and England, who led the

Stephen Jones searching for a gap against Agen.

attack? Stephen Jones. Similarly, it was his counter attack early in the second half against France in the Six Nations victory at the Stade de France (which led to Martyn Williams's try) that was the defining moment as far as our Grand Slam success was concerned. And at club and international level, he continues to create space for the sprinters in his teams: Rougerie, Paulse, the two Williamses and their like.

Allied to his attacking instincts is a fearless and fearsome defence, but the main weapon in his arsenal is his kicking ability where, unlike many of his peers, he seems comfortable on either foot. Small wonder that he is considered to be the premier scoring machine of his day, given his 317 points in the *Championnat* during season 2004/05.

Little wonder that selection for the British Lions followed and that rugby newspaper *Midi Olympique's* decided to name him the outstanding outside half in France during season 2004/05, an accolade which he particularly treasures.

So a new dawn beckons in the Massif Central of France. The powers-that-be at Clermont are acutely aware that Stephen Jones is the player who can help bring about the success they crave. I quote several Clermont supporters during a recent visit to the city made famous by Michelin's investments: 'Not only is he a truly great player, but a magnificent ambassador for your country.' Who knows he could end up as Mayor of Clermont Ferrand!

A Scarlet through-and-through in the blue shirt of Clermont.

58

Important decisions – past and present

The past: regaining ownership of Stradey Park.

I was around six years of age at the time: Everest had been conquered, Cardiff and Wales had both beaten the New Zealand All Blacks, Marilyn Monroe had made the front cover of 'Playboy' magazine and Dylan Thomas was lying on his death bed in St Vincent's Hospital, New York City. I cannot recall with any degree of detail any more about these newsworthy events but what remains crystal clear is the afternoon I spent at Bertram Mills Circus in Swansea.

Now in those days a visit to the circus was the highlight of the school holidays. This was before the television era, when the radio, the weekly comic, Meccano and the occasional packet of Parma Violets proved the only source of amusement for a six-year-old. I could hardly contain my excitement as we made our way into the big top. This feeling of expectation was heightened when the lights were dimmed, the music faded and the packed audience suddenly went deathly quiet. In an instant, two powerful spotlights picked out the figures of two acrobats swinging lazily on the trapeze high up in the rafters of the marquee. According to the circus programme, these were the best in the world, had been hired at great expense and were such experienced performers that they did not need to use a safety net.

Minutes into the routine, one of the acrobats plummeted to the ground and lay prostrate in front of us. (We were later to learn that he had been killed in the fall). Before anyone in the audience had time to draw breath, the ring was filled with clowns, jugglers and at least a dozen galloping white horses. The acrobat's body was unceremoniously carried outside and the show went on as if nothing untoward had taken place. The philosophy was, 'The show must go on.'

This was the mantra adopted by Llanelli Rugby Club in 1997 when the future looked particularly bleak. Two years earlier, rugby had bidden farewell to the amateur era with the dawning of a new professional era. For some English and French clubs, this truly was a new beginning. They benefited from the generous donations of wealthy benefactors and lucrative investments from multinational companies. This was not the case at Llanelli. Despite many promises of money from more than one source, this was not forthcoming. It has to be remembered that although officially the game was now a professional one, many clubs up and down the land were still being run by amateurs. Although these people had given of their time and effort over the years, this was not enough to cope with the demands of the new era.

It was also at this time that many of the big-name rugby players were in the market for lucrative contracts which would see out their playing days and would set them up financially once those days were over. Like many rugby committees all over Britain, Llanelli Rugby Club made some very unwise recruitment decisions, signing players whose salaries plunged them into huge debt. One such example was the decision to sign Frano Botica, the former All Black outside half and latterly one of the stars of Wigan Rugby League Club. Frano left Orrell and signed a contract with the Scarlets that would have been the envy of several Premiership footballers. This was a financial disaster for Llanelli and one which entailed a major review of the club's business plan.

It has to be said that on the field of play Botica proved a success. He played his first game at Stradey on October 1, 1996 and his tenure of almost two years at the club proved to be popular with fans – he played in 42 games and scored a total of 447 points. What is more, Botica's experience also helped the development of many young players at Llanelli, notably Stephen Jones.

Although the faithful still came through the turnstiles on a regular basis, it wasn't enough to rescue it from the financial quagmire in which it now found itself. The banks were also feeling a little nervous and were keen to recoup their investments. The only solution to the problem was to sell Stradey Park to the Welsh Rugby Union for the sum of £1.25 million.

An appeal was immediately launched in a bid to save the club. The financial situation was made public so that the supporters were aware of the gravity of the situation. It was immediately decided that a group of people, comprising former players, businessmen, accountants and lawyers would be formed to deal with the crisis. Thanks to the decisions made by the Chairman of this group, Ron Jones, together with the Chief Executive, Stuart Gallacher, the pressure was lifted and Llanelli RFC was able to put its finances in order.

Coupled with these decisions were those that saw the development of local rugby talent as opposed to the buying in of big-name players. The good times soon returned to Stradey Park, Llanelli was again in the news and silverware continued to overload the display cabinets. Added to this were some memorable performances in the Heineken Cup which proved a tonic for players and supporters alike.

At the time of writing, the club continues to flourish. The financial situation remains relatively solvent and the board under the chairmanship of Huw Evans operates effectively. One has to remember, however, the frailty of the situation during that period in 1996/97. Those people who helped salvage the club from its crisis have nothing but praise for the enthusiasm and determination of its supporters. Certainly, there was a great deal of disquiet regarding the situation, but instead of romanticising about the past they decided on a positive course of action – and they succeeded. After all, 'the show must go on.'

The present: It's goodbye to Stradey.

Expectations were high. The Member of Parliament could hardly contain his excitement. He had been the one chosen to escort the charismatic Indian leader, Mahatma Gandhi, on his tour of London and the surrounding area. This would be an ideal opportunity to show off the modern rail and road network, the high standards of living, and the freedoms enjoyed by the people at large. At the end of the two-day visit, Gandhi was asked, 'As a result of your visit, what do you think of Western civilization?' Quick as a flash came the answer, 'I think it would be a very good idea.' That was the end of the conversation – or at least the MP's reaction has never been recorded.

What has this to do with Stradey Park, I hear you ask. Simply this: we are often so caught up in our own concerns, that we do not see the bigger picture. If, however, we view things from a different perspective, we can often make decisions which can, although uncomfortable or trying at the time, produce a positive conclusion.

Stradey Park has been home to Llanelli Rugby Football Club for well over a century. Situated as it is between the town centre and the village of Pwll, it has become part of the history and folklore of the area. Battles have been fought and won on this hallowed ground and it is here that the giants of the rugby world have displayed their talents. It is for these reasons, above all others, that I sympathise wholeheartedly with those who maintain that it is here that Llanelli should continue playing rugby. For some it is an indisputable fact that the two cannot be separated.

However, it is time to consign sentiment to the history books. No one can argue that Stradey Park is not a relic of the past: outdated, shabby and generally run down. I think the Board at Llanelli RFC, working in tandem with Carmarthenshire County Council, should be applauded for their vision in sanctioning the move to a new campus. After all, in 2005, Llanelli is not only seen as a town team, but also a regional one representing West, Mid and North Wales. It is fitting, therefore, that it should have a stadium worthy of this new status.

In the era of the Heineken Cup when we regularly visit and host European clubs, one cannot fail to compare and contrast what they have to offer. Brive, the French club, for example has its rugby field centred in the middle of a multi-faceted campus where there is also an athletics track, tennis courts, a football field, training grounds and excellent parking facilities – all run by the town council. The main focus of the complex is the rugby stadium with its impressive stands, a setting which brings the club into the new millennium.

The same is repeated all over France in towns and cities such as Agen, Narbonne, Montpellier, Pau, Lyons and Dax where the sports clubs are all keen to take advantage of the facilities provided by the various municipal councils; a service which is seen to benefit the whole community.

'It is not enough to have a good mind. The main thing is to use it well.' These words belong to the French philosopher René Descartes, and it is obvious that they have been an inspiration to his fellow Frenchmen and their municipal councillors. It is heartening to see that Carmarthenshire County Council is following suit.

59

Panache and finesse

The Scarlet way

It was the Reverend T.J. Davies who once said, *'Does neb yn gadael ôl traed ar dywod amser wrth eistedd ar ei ben-ôl'* – no one leaves a footprint on the sands of time by sitting on one's backside! As a nation, we find it difficult to celebrate and enjoy a success story – especially, and perversely, if it happens to be one of our own. At the onset of a new rugby season, it is inevitable that several column inches and hours of air-time will be given over to speculating on what lies ahead for our teams in the months to come. There will be the usual criticisms reserved for the administrators, coaches and some players and there will be a lot of harking back to the glory days that have gone before. And a faction of former players will be amongst the most vocal in their carping. If these people who voice these opinions transferred their energies into actually taking an active part in proceedings, then maybe they would be able to make a difference. There are those people who 'do' and there are those who 'talk about doing' without actually accomplishing anything. As T.J. said, we are a nation who sit on our backsides.

In any age, in any field, there will always be found individuals with a pioneering spirit and there are few more celebrated than Frank Lloyd Wright, the American architect whose forefathers hailed from Cardiganshire. It was he who was responsible for the design of the Guggenheim Museum in New York City. A few weeks before the official opening in 1959, the curator contacted Mr Wright's office to inform him of a slight structural problem they had encountered. He tried to put the matter as delicately as possible: 'Sir, the building is an architectural gem. However, there's one slight problem; the cargo doors are too small. We can't get the art work in!' The architect's answer was brief and to the point – 'Well, cut the art work in half!'

Perfection in sport is nigh on impossible. Sufficient ambition, dedication and expertise can, however, make excellence attainable and sustainable. One who aims for excellence every time is the Australian swimmer, Ian Thorpe. Some six months before the start of the 2002 Commonwealth Games at Manchester, he contacted the authorities wanting to know the exact distance from the athletes' village to the swimming pool. An e-mail confirmed the distance to be 1.6km. So for the months leading up to the Games, Thorpe would park his car 1.6km from the Aquatic Centre in Sydney and walk there each day for his training sessions. No one could wish for a more professional attention to detail.

Duncan Fletcher, the England and Wales cricket coach, has been an inspirational influence on the Test side over the past few seasons. He is credited with invoking a more professional attitude amongst the players. They are now seen to perform as a unit, both on and off the field. Therein lies the strength of the Llanelli rugby squad. Over the years Gareth Jenkins has united them as a team, instilled in them a fierce competitive spirit and a desire to play the kind of rugby which pleases the supporters. He is a master motivator.

As a country with 2.5 million inhabitants, we are unlikely to conquer the world of rugby. But with hard work, perseverance and a little bit of good fortune, a national XV can from time to time win Grand Slams and create major upsets in World Cups; Welsh regions in the not too distant future can win the Heineken Cup. However, changing attitudes leading to no-risk on-field polices and never-ending pre-planned playing sequences have all combined to produce fewer opportunities for the creative individuals.

Gareth Jenkins putting pressure on the All Blacks' scrum half, Lyn Colling,
during the famous victory in 1972.

During the past century Brazilian footballers, West Indian cricketers and French rugby players have all managed to play the game (and win) with a degree of flair, finesse and panache. This has also been the Llanelli way, and it is imperative that the club continues to excite in a way which it has traditionally done since its inception way back in 1875.

60

A sense of belonging

Emblazoned above the entrance gates to Anfield, home of Liverpool F.C., are the words 'You'll never walk alone'. This mantra has served the club well over several decades and invokes in staff and supporters alike a feeling of belonging. Indeed, such was this depth of feeling that it drew criticism from some quarters that the club was somewhat introspective, relying too much on its own personnel and re-employing from within its own ranks.

The classic example of this was seen in the long line of former players who subsequently became coaches at Anfield. Bill Shankly, Bob Paisley, Joe Fagan, Kenny Dalglish, Roy Evans and Graeme Souness were initially employed not so much for their coaching skills but because of their loyalty to the club and their affinity with Anfield and the Kop. That they made such a success of their new careers says much about the quality of their character and immense pride in their work.

There are many similarities between Liverpool F.C. and Llanelli RFC. Apart from the obvious fact that both teams played in shades of red, the Scarlets' supporters faithfully follow their team with as much enthusiasm and commitment as any demonstrated on the Kop. They feel a part of the set-up and there is reason to believe that the blood flowing through their veins is in fact scarlet and not red!

And again, as with the Merseyside club, many of the administrators at Stradey are former players. The Team Manager is Anthony Buchanan, a former Scarlet prop forward who hails from Ystradgynlais. His playing career bridged the Eighties and Nineties when he won five Welsh caps – against Tonga at Palmerston North, England and New Zealand at Brisbane, Australia in Rotorua and Ireland in Dublin. Those eagle-eyed readers may have noted that not one of these caps was won on home soil!

The Llanelli coaches have been recognised in other chapters but again like Anfield, Stradey has always depended on a team of loyal volunteers and back-room staff to keep operations moving efficiently. In an emotional speech delivered on the steps of Liverpool City Hall after the team had won yet another trophy, Bill Shankly paid tribute to his staff. He thanked the groundsmen, the programme sellers, the kit man, those responsible for washing the kit, those who cleared the terraces of rubbish and the tea ladies. In fact, he thanked everyone except the players. He wanted all concerned to be aware that the 'team' was not only made up of the eleven who kicked the ball around the field, but wanted to emphasise the importance of a team ethic.

Llanelli was one of the first rugby clubs in Europe to employ a dedicated fitness coach. At the end of the Sixties, Tom Hudson from the University of

Bath was appointed to take charge of the players' fitness requirements. He was followed in the Eighties and Nineties by Peter Herbert who was rightly credited for maintaining fitness levels that kept players firing on all cylinders throughout the season.

The present fitness coach, Wayne Proctor, is again a former player. Born in Cardigan, Wayne is amongst those who regard Stradey Park as their spiritual home. During his schooldays, most of Wayne's free time was spent on the athletics track where he developed into a 400-metre runner of some distinction. The time spent cultivating his running skills stood him in good stead when he later transferred to rugby. He was a natural footballer comfortable in both attack and defence and a rock when asked to gather the high ball. His speed, of course, was his main asset and led to 11 international tries in 37 appearances.

To complete the team of home-grown talent is Stuart Gallacher, the present Chief Executive of the club. His playing days at Stradey came to an end in the early Seventies when he joined the professional ranks. As well as his administrative role with the Scarlets, Stuart also represents Wales on the board of the ERC – a duty he takes seriously in his quest to secure a successful future for the Scarlets and the other Welsh regions.

Llanelli's programme was the Best in Britain, 1992/93.
Roy Bergiers (in the middle) honouring its editor, Les Williams.
On the right: Edward James (Club president) –
the man who silenced John McEnroe at Wimbledon.

61

Thanks to the fans

Failure is not fatal. Only failure to get back up is.

John C. Maxwell

There have been several instances in this book where I have compared the sports field to the theatre. Is not the pitch like a stage, after all? Then there are the players, the support staff, and last, but by no means least, the audience. It is the latter who create the atmosphere, inspire the performers and who help in the creation of the stars. There would be no joy whatsoever for a Ryan Giggs, a Simon Jones, a Bryn Terfel, a Ioan Gruffudd or a Dwayne Peel in playing to an empty house.

Those faithful supporters on the Tanner Bank are just as important as any others the world over. Their partisan support of the team is legendary and is part of Stradey's magic. Here there is a natural mixture of devotees of both sexes and all ages, united in one goal – giving voice in support of their team.

Traditionally the half-time whistle at Stradey had been the signal for a pitch invasion from the younger members of the crowd. They swarmed around the players like bees around a honey pot listening to the team talk and jostling for autographs. The poet and Chaired Bard Ceri Wyn Jones composed a verse on the very subject recalling his boyhood experience of being able to touch Phil Bennett's shirt.

Roedd pob un sosban yn lanach, rywsut,	Each saucepan's sheen was cleaner, all in all
pob un crys yn gochach,	the scarlet was redder,
a'i laswellt gymaint glasach	the green grass so much greener
pan dwtshes i Benni bach.	when I touched Phil Bennett here.

In the new age of health and safety, this practice has sadly been barred. The law came into force on September 25, 2004, and in their own indomitable fashion the Scarlets' supporters responded – by running onto the field at half-time! It will be interesting to see if this practice continues in the new stadium. It was also Ceri Wyn Jones who reiterated what many aficionados already felt: 'Stradey Park is the spiritual home of all Welsh-speaking followers of the game', the Mecca of the West. This feeling of being Welsh has been an integral part of Llanelli RFC since its inception. The name of the visiting teams is displayed in the native tongue on the scoreboard; the song *'Sosban Fach'* has been adopted as the team anthem and the players take to the field to the strains of Dafydd Iwan's *'Yma o Hyd'*, leaving no one in any doubt of the club's patriotism. Indeed, as the poet W.R. Evans in his autobiography wrote in his rich, native Pembrokeshire dialect:

Ma' pwer o ddŵr berw Hen Wlad 'y Nhade   From Land of my Fathers' deepest cauldron
In sosban Llanelli ar Barc y Strade.   comes the boiling water of Stradey's saucepan.

There is, however, room for improvement. The use of the language in match-day programmes is almost non-existent and with so many eloquent writers amongst its supporters, perhaps it is time these people were invited to make a contribution. There is also a reluctance to adopt a bilingual policy over the PA system – Glamorgan County Cricket Club have shown the way in this respect by ensuring a sense of fair play to both languages.

There has been talk of late of 'scouring the world for talent'. Llanelli RFC throughout the last one-hundred-and-thirty years has provided a launching pad for some of Wales's greatest ever players and coaches – Ernie, Albert, Ivor, Carwyn, Delme, Phil, Ray, Gareth, Ieuan, Dwayne and many others were all born and bred just a few miles from the ground. The club must not forget its past. And not forget that, as Elber Hubbard said, 'It does not take much strength to do things, but it requires great strength to decide on what to do.'

Yes, we will also miss Stradey when the Scarlets play in their new stadium, but as Gareth Charles claims in his foreword to this book – 'It will be a new theatre, but the dream remains the same.' It is hoped that the same spirit exists on this new stage, behind the scenes and in the new auditorium, and that the Welsh language, as well as the success on the field, lives on for generations to come as the words *'Ry'n ni yma o hyd'* ('We're still here') continue to ring in the ears of the supporters.